ISBN 978-1-333-48786-7
PIBN 10510705

1 MONTH OF
FREE
READING

at
www.ForgottenBooks.com

By purchasing this book you are eligible for one month membership to ForgottenBooks.com, giving you unlimited access to our entire collection of over 700,000 titles via our web site and mobile apps.

To claim your free month visit:

www.forgottenbooks.com/free510705

English
Français
Deutsche
Italiano
Español
Português

www.forgottenbooks.com

Mythology Photography **Fiction**
Fishing Christianity **Art** Cooking
Essays Buddhism Freemasonry
Medicine **Biology** Music **Ancient
Egypt** Evolution Carpentry Physics
Dance Geology **Mathematics** Fitness
Shakespeare **Folklore** Yoga Marketing
Confidence Immortality Biographies
Poetry **Psychology** Witchcraft
Electronics Chemistry History **Law**
Accounting **Philosophy** Anthropology
Alchemy Drama Quantum Mechanics
Atheism Sexual Health **Ancient History**
Entrepreneurship Languages Sport
Paleontology Needlework Islam
Metaphysics Investment Archaeology
Parenting Statistics Criminology
Motivational

THE

MASONIC HARP:

A COLLECTION OF

Masonic Odes, Hymns, Songs, &c.

FOR THE PUBLIC AND PRIVATE

Ceremonies and Festivals

OF THE

FRATERNITY.

By GEORGE W. CHASE, K. T.

EDITOR OF MASONIC JOURNAL, &C.

BOSTON:

PREFACE.

Believing the Masonic Fraternity have long wanted, and would liberally patronize, a complete and *practical* collection of Music for the various public and private Ceremonies and Festivals of the Order, the compiler of the following pages has been for several years collecting material for such a work, and now presents, as the result of his labors, *The Masonic Harp*, in the hope that it will be found adapted to the purpose. That the work is faultless, he does not for a moment suppose, but that it is many steps in advance of any heretofore published for the purpose, he fully believes. His desire has been to furnish a *complete collection of appropriate Odes, Hymns*, &c., for all ordinary Masonic Occasions, and if he has failed in his effort, he will still have the satisfaction of knowing that "it was in his *heart*" to present a *good work.*

With very few exceptions, the tunes in the *Harp* are those which have become established favorites, and are widely known and admired. It was for this reason they were selected. In arranging them for Masonic use, much care has been taken to give the Melody and Bass as they are most universally known, and with this view, not one note of either has been knowingly changed.

Believing that the Craft stood in need of a much larger variety of Odes and Hymns of a *devotional* character, the compiler has "adapted" more than *one hundred* such, from various authors, and hopes they will prove acceptable.

The insertion of a complete "Masonic Burial Service," and also a "Burial Service for the Orders of Knighthood," will be found not only convenient for such occasions, but will add much to the interest and general effect of such services.

Many of the Hymns and Odes marked "Opening" will answer equally as well for "Closing," and *vice versa;* and many of those marked for a particular degree, are nearly or quite as appropriate for some other degrees. The Chorister (and every Masonic Body should have one) will take this fact into consideration when making his selections.

Most of the Tunes have several sets of verses appropriate for them, upon the same and facing pages, which will ordinarily afford a sufficient variety for the various occasions; but, if necessary, the use of two books by each singer, (as in Church Choirs,) will add a ten or even twenty fold greater range for selection, and must prove amply sufficient for all practical purposes.

The Compiler acknowledges his great obligations to Mr. Samuel M. Downs, of this place, for his assistance in arranging Music for *The Harp*, and for his original compositions, which give additional value to the work; and also to Bros. Rob. Morris, J. B. Taylor, Cornelius Moore, and others, for their kind permission to use many of their excellent compositions.

With the hope that the use of the Hymns and Odes contained in it, will add to the interest and effect of the beautiful ceremonies of the Fraternity, and meet their approval, *The Masonic Harp* is now presented.

G. W. C.

Haverhill, Mass

INDEX TO MUSIC.

INDEX TO SUBJECTS.

[1*]

INDEX OF FIRST LINES.

MASONIC HARP.

ROCKINGHAM. L. M.

OPENING HYMN.

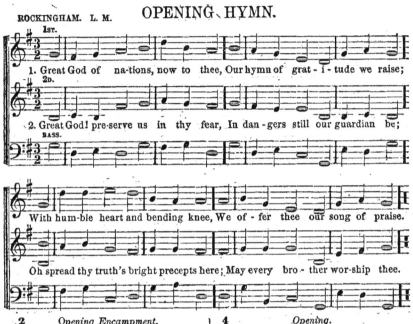

1. Great God of na-tions, now to thee, Our hymn of grat-i-tude we raise;

2. Great God! pre-serve us in thy fear, In dan-gers still our guardian be;

With hum-ble heart and bending knee, We of-fer thee our song of praise.

Oh spread thy truth's bright precepts here; May every bro-ther wor-ship thee.

2 *Opening Encampment.*

1 The peace which God alone reveals,
  And by his word of grace imparts,
  Which only the believer feels,
  Direct, and keep, and cheer our hearts.

2 And may the holy Three in One,
  The Father, Word, and Comforter,
  Pour an abundant blessing down
  On every soul assembled here.

3 *Opening.*

1 How blest the sacred tie, that binds
  In sweet communion kindred minds!
  How swift the heavenly course they run,
  Whose hearts, whose faith, whose hopes
    are one!

2 Together oft they seek the place
  Where Friendship smiles on every face;
  How high, how strong their raptures swell,
  There's none but kindred souls can tell.

3 Nor shall the glowing flame expire,
  When dimly burns frail nature's fire;
  Then shall they meet in realms above —
  A heaven of joy, a heaven of love.

4 *Opening.*

1 Bless, O my soul, the living God,
  Call home thy thoughts that rove abroad;
  Let all the powers within me join,
  In work and worship so divine.

2 Eternal are thy mercies, Lord;
  Eternal truth attends thy word;
  Thy praise shall sound from shore to shore,
  Till suns shall rise and set no more.

5 *Opening.*

1 From east to west, o'er land and sea,
  Where brothers meet, and friends agree,
  Let incense rise from hearts sincere,
  The dearest offering gathered here.

2 Our trust reposed in God alone,
  Who ne'er will contrite hearts disown;
  Our faith shall mark that holy light,
  Whose beams our dearest joys unite.

6 *Opening.*

Be thou exalted, O our God,
Above the heavens, where angels dwell;
Thy power on earth be known abroad,
And land to land thy wonders tell.

OLD HUNDRED. L. M.

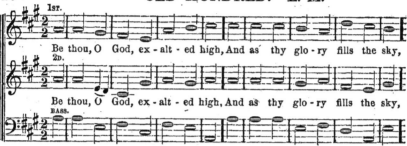

Be thou, O God, ex-alt-ed high, And as' thy glo-ry fills the sky,

Be thou, O God, ex-alt-ed high, And as' thy glo-ry fills the sky,

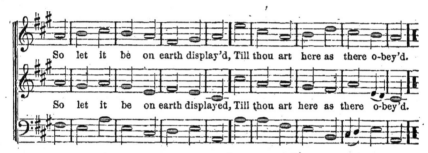

So let it be on earth display'd, Till thou art here as there o-bey'd.

So let it be on earth displayed, Till thou art here as there o-bey'd.

8   *Mark Master. Work.*

1 Another six days work is done;
Another Sabbath is begun;
Return, my soul! enjoy thy rest!
Improve the day thy God hath blessed.

2 In holy duties let the day —
In holy pleasures pass away!
How sweet a Sabbath thus to spend,
In hope of one that ne'er shall end!

9   *Closing Hymn.*

1 Come, brothers, ere to-night we part,
Join every voice and every heart;
One solemn hymn to God we'll raise,
One closing song of grateful praise.

2 Here, brothers, we may meet no more,
But there is yet a happier shore;
And there, released from toil and pain,
Dear brothers, we shall meet again.

10   *Mark Master. Closing.*

1 Accept, Great Builder of the skies,
Our heart-felt acts of sacrifice!
Each brother found a living stone,
While bending low before Thy throne.

2 While Craftsmen true their work prepare,
With thoughts unstained, and holy care,
May each be fitly formed, and placed
Where LOVE DIVINE his hopes had traced.

11   *Dedication Ode.**

1 Great Architect of heaven and earth,
To whom all nature owes its birth;
Thou spoke! and vast creation stood,
Surveyed the work — pronounced it good.

2 Lord, can'st thou deign to own and bless
This humble dome, this sacred place?
Oh! let thy spirit's presence shine
Within these walls — this house of thine.

3 'Twas reared in honor of thy name;
Here kindle, Lord, the sacred flame:
Oh! make it burn in every heart,
And never from this place depart.

4 Lord, here the wants of all supply,
And fit our souls to dwell on high;
From service in this humble place,
Raise us to praise thee face to face.

12   *Royal Arch. Closing.*

1 Almighty Father! heavenly King,
Before whose Sacred Name we bend,
Accept the praises which we sing,
And to our humble prayer attend

2 Grant us, great God! thy powerful aid
To guide us through this vale of tears;
Oh let thy goodness be displayed,
To soothe the mind, and calm our fears.

* Suitable also for opening or closing a Lodge

13 *Initiation, or Raising.*

1 Dangers of every form attend
  Your steps, as onward you proceed;
No earthly power can now befriend,
Or aid you in this time of need.

2 Confide your trust in him alone,
  Who rules all things above, below;
Send your petitions to his throne,
For he alone can help you now.

14 *Dedication Masonic Hall.*

1 Genius of Masonry, descend,
  And with thee bring thy spotless train;
Constant our sacred rites attend,
  While we adore thy peaceful reign.

(Dedication to Freemasonry.)

2 Bring with thee Virtue, brightest maid;
  Bring Love, bring Truth, and Friendship here,
While kind Relief will lend her aid,
  To smooth the wrinkled brow of care.

(Dedication to Virtue.)

3 Come Charity, with goodness crowned,
  Encircled in thy heavenly robe;
Diffuse thy blessings all around,
  To every corner of the globe.

(Dedication to Universal Benevolence.)

4 To Heaven's high Architect all praise,
  All praise, all gratitude be given,
Who deigned the human soul to raise,
By mystic secrets sprung from heaven.

15 *Closing Hymn.*

1 Once more, O Lord, let grateful praise,
  From every heart to thee ascend;
Thou art the guardian of our days,
  Our first, our best, and changeless friend.

2 Hear, now, our parting hymn of praise,
  And bind our hearts in love divine;
O, may we walk in wisdom's ways,
And ever feel that we are thine.

16 *Opening, or Closing.*

1 Great Lord of earth, and seas, and skies!
  Thy wealth the needed world supplies;
And safe beneath thy guardian arm,
We live secured from every harm.

2 To thee we cheerful homage bring;
In grateful hymns thy praises sing;
On thee we ever will depend,
Thou art our sure, our faithful friend.

17 *Opening.*

1 Help us to praise thee, Lord of light,
  Help us thy boundless love declare;
And while we look to thee this night,
  Aid us, and hearken to our prayer.

2 Thy light upon our evening pour;
  Oh! may our souls no sunset see;
But death to us an open door
  Of an eternal morning be.

18 *Anniversary Ode.*

1 Hail! Masonry, thou craft divine!
  Come, Brethren, let us cheerful join,
To celebrate this happy day,
And homage to our Master pay.

2 Next sing, my muse, our Warden's praise,
  With chorus loud, in tuneful lays;
Oh! may these columns ne'er decay,
  Until the world dissolves away.

3 Come, Brethren cheerful, join with me,
  To sing the praise of Masonry;
The noble, faithful, and the brave,
Whose Art shall live beyond the grave.

19 *Initiation, or Crafting.*

1 Thus far the Lord has led me on;
  Thus far his power prolongs my days;
And every evening shall make known
Some fresh memorial of his grace.

2 Oh! may his love, with sweet control,
  Bind every passion of my soul;
Bid every vain desire depart,
And dwell forever in my heart.

20 *Opening, or Closing.*

1 Now let my soul, eternal King,
  To thee its grateful tribute bring;
My knee with humble homage bow,
My tongue perform its solemn vow.

2 Oh let my heart, oh let my song,
  Through endless years thy praise prolong;
Let distant climes thy name adore,
Till time and nature are no more.

21 *Installation, or Dedication.*

1 Almighty Ruler of the skies,
  Through all the earth thy name is spread,
And thine eternal glories rise
  Above the heavens thy hands have made.

2 To thee the voices of the young
  Their grateful notes of honor raise;
And babes, with uninstructed tongue,
Declare the wonders of thy praise.

3 Eternal God! celestial King!
  Exalted be thy glorious name;
Let hosts in heaven thy praises sing,
  And all on earth thy love proclaim.

THE GREAT LIGHT.

UXBRIDGE. L. M.
1ST.

OPENING.

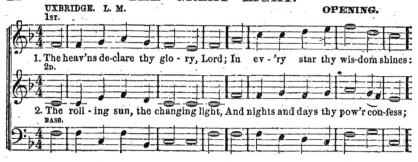

1. The heav'ns de-clare thy glo - ry, Lord; In ev - 'ry star thy wis-dom shines:

2D.

2. The roll - ing sun, the changing light, And nights and days thy pow'r con-fess;

BASS.

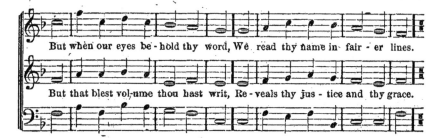

But when our eyes be - hold thy word, We read thy name in fair - er lines.

But that blest vol-ume thou hast writ, Re - veals thy jus - tice and thy grace.

23   *Initiation.*

1 Far from the world's cold strife and pride,
   Come join our peaceful, happy band;
 Come, stranger, we your feet will guide,
    Where truth and love shall hold com-
      mand.

2 Although in untried paths you tread,
   And filled, perhaps, with anxious fear;
 A brother's faithful hand shall lead
   Where doubt and darkness disappear.

3 Here may you in our labors join,
   And prove yourself a brother true;
 All sordid, selfish cares resign,
   And keep our sacred truths in view.

24   *Closing.*

1 Come, brothers, ere to-night we part,
 Join every voice and every heart;
 One solemn hymn to God we'll raise,
 One closing song of grateful praise.

2 Here, brothers, we may meet no more,
 But there is yet a happier shore;
 And there, released from toil and pain,
 Dear brothers, we shall meet again.

25   *Opening.*

1 Eternal source of every joy!
 Well may thy praise our lips employ,
 While in thy temple we appear,
 Whose goodness crowns the circling year.

2 Wide as the wheels of nature roll,
 Thy hand supports and guides the whole!
 The sun is taught by thee to rise,
 And darkness when to veil the skies.

3 Seasons, and months, and weeks, and days,
 Demand successive songs of praise;
 And be the grateful homage paid,
 With morning light and evening shade.

26   *Closing.*

1 Once more, O Lord, let grateful praise,
   In songs of joy to thee ascend;
 Thou art the guardian of our days,
   Our first, our best and changeless friend.

2 Hear, now, our parting hymn of praise,
   And bind our hearts in love divine;
 O, may we walk in wisdom's ways,
   And ever feel that we are thine.

27   *Installation, or Dedication.*

1 Ye happy few, who here extend
In perfect lines, from east to west,
With fervent zeal the Lodge defend,
And lock its secrets in each breast.

2 Since ye are met upon the square,
Bid love and friendship jointly reign;
Be peace and harmony your care,
Nor break the adamantine chain.

3 Behold the planets, how they move,
Yet keep due order as they run;
Then imitate the stars above,
And shine resplendent as the sun.

4. Then let us celebrate the praise
Of all who have enriched the art;
Let gratitude our voices raise,
And each true brother bear a part.

28   *Opening.*

1 Genius of Masonry descend,
In mystic numbers while we sing;
Enlarge our souls, the craft defend,
And hither all thy influence bring.

2 Oh may our voice to Friendship move;
Be Virtue ours in all its parts;
Let Justice, Harmony, and Love,
Come and possess our faithful hearts.

29   *Anniversary.*

1 Ye gracious powers of choral song,
Attend; inspire your festive throng;
Let harmless mirth, and frolic glee,
Dance sportive at our jubilee.

2 We ask no sound of spear or shield,
No trophies of the ensanguined field;
Let Hope, let Faith, and Charity,
Begin and end our jubilee.

3 Then call from east to west the world,
The mystic banners are unfurled!
And oh! departed ancients, see
From heaven, and bless our jubilee!

4 Be this the general, cordial toast,
A wish that never should be lost,
That all the world may Masons be,
And live and love in jubilee.

[2]

30   *Opening.*

With all my powers of heart and tongue,
I'll praise my Maker in my song;
Angels shall hear the notes I raise,
Approve the song, and join the praise.

31   *Opening.*

1 What joy, when brethren dwell combined,
Inspiring unity of mind;
'Tis like the sacred unction shed,
On Aaron's venerable head;
When bathed in fragrance, doth respire
His rev'rend beard and rich attire.

2 Like dews, which, trickling from the sky,
In pearly drops on Hermon lie;
Or balmy vapors, which distill
On Zion's consecrated hill;
For there the Lord his blessing placed,
And these with life eternal graced.

32   *Fellow Craft.*

1 Hail, Masonry, thou Craft divine!
Glory of earth, from heaven revealed;
Which doth with jewels precious shine,
From all but Masons' eyes concealed.

2 From scorching heat, from piercing cold,
From beasts whose roar the forest rends,
From the assaults of warriors bold,
The Mason's art mankind defends.

3 Sweet fellowship, from envy free,
Friendly converse of brotherhood,
The Lodge's lasting cement be,
Which has for ages firmly stood.

33   *Funeral Hymn.*

1 Unveil thy bosom, faithful tomb,
Take this new treasure to thy trust,
And give these sacred relics room
To slumber in the silent dust.

2 Nor pain, nor grief, nor anxious fear,
Invade thy bounds; no mortal woes
Can reach the silent sleepers here,
And Angels watch their soft repose.

3 So Jesus slept; God's dying Son,
Passed through the grave, and blest the bed;
Rest here, dear Saint, 'till from his throne
The morning break, and pierce the shade.

4 Break from thy throne, illustrious Morn;
Attend, O Earth, his sovereign word;
Restore thy trust, a glorious form;
Let him ascend to meet his Lord.

DUKE ST. L. M.
1st.

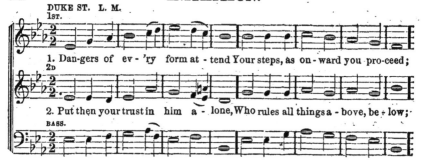

1. Dan-gers of ev-'ry form at-tend Your steps, as on-ward you pro-ceed;

2. Put then your trust in him a-lone, Who rules all things a-bove, be-low;

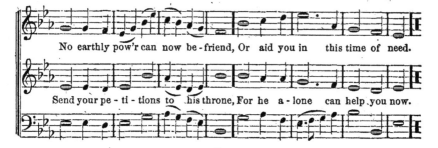

No earthly pow'r can now be-friend, Or aid you in this time of need.

Send your pe-ti-tions to his throne, For he a-lone can help you now.

35   *Dedication, or Opening.*

1 Pour out thy Spirit from on high;
   Lord! thine assembled servants bless;
Graces and gifts to each supply,
   And clothe us with thy righteousness.

2 Within this temple, where we stand
   To teach the truth as taught by Thee,
In favor bless this chosen band,
   With Wisdom, Strength, and Unity.

3 Fervor and Zeal, freely impart;
   Firmness, with meekness from above,
That each may with a faithful heart,
   Here labor for the cause of Love.

4 And when our work is finished here,
   May we in Hope our charge resign:
When thou, Grand Master, shalt appear,
   May we and all mankind be thine.

36   *Opening, or Initiation.*

1 Lord, while we here our work prepare,
   With thoughts unstained, and holy care,
May each be fitly formed, and placed
Where *Love Divine* his hopes had traced.

37   *Closing.*

1 Brothers, with pleasure let us part,
Since we are of one mind and heart;
No length of days, or distant place,
Can ever break these bands of grace.

2 Parting with joy, we'll join and sing
The wonders of our Lord and King;
Our bodies distant may remove,
But nothing shall divide our love.

3 A few more rolling days and years,
Shall end our labors, toils, and fears;
We soon shall reach that blissful shore,
Where parting shall be known no more.

38   *Opening.*

1 O Lord, behold before thy throne,
   A band of brothers lowly bend;
Thy face we seek, thy Name we own,
   And pray that thou wilt be our friend.

2 Grant us, we pray, a willing mind,
   To learn what thou would'st have us do,
And how we may thy favor find,
   And love and serve each other too.

39 *Opening, or Consecration.*

1 How blest the sacred tie, that binds
In sweet communion kindred minds!
How swift the heavenly course they run,
Whose hearts, whose faith, whose hopes
  are one.

2 Together oft they seek the place
Where Masons meet with smiling face;
How high, how strong their raptures swell,
There's none but kindred souls can tell.

3 Nor shall the glowing flame expire,
When dimly burns frail nature's fire;
Then shall they meet in realms above,
A heaven of joy, a heaven of love.

40 *Closing.*

1 Great God, we sing thy mighty hand;
By that supported still we stand:
The opening day thy mercy shows;
Let mercy crown it till it close.

2 When death shall close our earthly songs,
And seal in silence mortal tongues,
Oh thou, in whom we put our trust,
Receive us to thyself at last.

41 *Initiation, or Raising.*

1 Let us remember, in our youth,
  Before the evil days draw nigh,
Our *Great Creator* and his *Truth!*
  Ere memory fail, and pleasure fly;
Or sun, or moon, or planet's light
  Grow dark, or clouds return in gloom;
Ere vital spark no more incite,
  When strength shall bow, and years consume.

2 Let us in youth remember *Him!*
Who formed our frame, and spirits gave,
Ere windows of the mind grow dim,
  Or door of speech obstructed wave;
When voice of bird fresh terrors wake,
  And music's daughters charm no more,
Or fear to rise, with trembling shake,
  Along the path we travel o'er.

3 In youth, to God let memory cling,
  Before desire shall fail, or wane,
Or e'er be loosed life's silver string,
  Or bowl at fountain rent in twain;
For man to his long home doth go,
  And mourners group around his urn;
Our dust to dust again must flow,
  And spirits unto God return.

42 *Hymn for Opening.*

1 Master Supreme! accept our praise;
  Still bless this consecrated band;
Parent of Light! illume our ways,
  And guide us by thy sovereign hand.

2 May Faith, Hope, Charity, divine,
  Here hold their undivided reign;
Friendship and Harmony combine
  To soothe our cares, to banish pain.

3 May Pity dwell within each breast,
  Relief attend the suffering poor;
Thousands by this, our Lodge, be blest,
  Till worth, distress'd, shall want no more.

43 *Initiation.*

1 Far from the world's cold strife and pride,
  Come join our peaceful, happy band;
Come, stranger, we your feet will guide,
  Where Truth and Love shall hold command.

2 Although in untried paths you tread,
  And filled, perhaps, with anxious fear,
A brother's faithful hand shall lead,
  Where doubt and darkness disappear.

3 Then may you in our labors join,
  And prove yourself a brother true;
All sordid, selfish cares resign,
  And keep our sacred truths in view.

44 *Opening.*

1 From North to South, from East to West,
Advance the myriads of the blest;
From every clime of earth they come,
And find with us a common home.

2 In one immortal throng, we view
Pagan and Christian, Greek and Jew;
But all their doubt and darkness o'er,
One only God! they here adore.

45 *Opening.*

Oh! God of grace, before thy throne,
  Thy suppliants bow, with holy fear;
Those thou art pleased to call thine own,
  Invoke thy sacred presence here.

46 *Closing.*

1 Great God, to thee our closing song,
  With humble gratitude we raise;
Oh let thy mercy tune our tongue,
  And fill our hearts with lively praise.

2 Let Faith and Hope our eyelids close;
  With sleep refresh our feeble frame;
Safe in thy care may we repose,
  And wake with praises to thy name.

INITIATION.

From "CARMINA SÁCRA,". By permission.

WARD. L. M.

1st.

1. Thus far the Lord has led me on; Thus far his pow'r prolongs my days;

2d.

2. Much of my time has run to waste, And I, per - haps, am near my home;

BASS.

And ev -'ry evening shall make known Some fresh me - mo - rial of his grace.

But he for-gives my fol - lies past, And gives me strength for days to come.

48　　*Initiation.*

1 Far from the world's cold strife and pride,
　Come join our peaceful, happy band;
Come, stranger, we your feet will guide,
Where Truth and Love shall hold com-
　　mand.

2 Although in untried paths you tread,
　And filled, perhaps, with anxious fear,
A Brother's faithful hand shall lead
Where doubt and darkness disappear.

3 Then may you in our labors join,
　And prove yourself a Brother true;
All sordid, selfish cares resign,
And keep our sacred truths in view.

49　　*Opening.*

1 Come, all ye gentle springs that move
　And animate the human mind,
And by your energy improve
　The social bond by which we're joined.

2 This happy lodge, of care devoid,
　And haggard malice always free,
Shall by your aid be still employed
In social love and harmony

50　　*Opening.*

1 Pour out thy Spirit from on high;
　Lord! thine assembled servants bless;
Graces and gifts to each supply,
　And clothe us with thy righteousness.

2 Within this temple, where we stand
　To teach the Truth as taught by Thee,
In favor bless this chosen band,
　With Wisdom, Strength, and Unity.

3 And when our work is finished here,
　May we in Hope our charge resign:
When thou, Grand Master, shalt appear,
May we and all mankind be thine.

51　　*Master Mason.*

1 Dangers of every form attend
　Your steps, as onward you proceed;
No earthly power can now befriend,
　Or aid you in this time of need.

2 Then put your trust in Him alone,
　Who rules all things above, below;
Send your petitions to his throne,
　For he alone can help you now.

52   *Opening.*

1 Away from every worldly care,
  In this fraternal, loved retreat;
We leave this troubled world afar,
  And wait and worship near thy seat.

2 Lord, in this temple of thy grace,
  We feel thy presence, and adore;
We gaze upon thy lovely face,
  And learn the wonders of thy power.

3 Here let our faith in Thee abide;
  Forever firm thy justice stands;
Not all the powers of earth beside,
  Can e'er dissolve the sacred bands.

53   *Opening.*

1 From busy scenes we now retreat,
  To hold converse, O God, with thee;
While bowing low before Thy feet,
  Let this the "gate of heaven" be.

2 Teach us to know and love thy way,
  By thine unerring guidance led;
And grant, to life's remotest day,
  Our willing feet thy paths may tread.

54 *Masonic Hymn.*—J. H. SHEPPARD.

1 Ah! when shall we three meet like them,
  Who last were at Jerusalem?
For one lies low, alas! he's not,
  The green Accacia marks the spot.

2 Though poor he was, with kings he trod;
  Though great, he humbly knelt to God:
Ah! when shall hope restore again,
  The broken link of friendship's chain.

3 Behold! where mourning beauty bent,
  In silence o'er his monument,
And wildly spread, in sorrow there,
  The ringlets of her flowing hair.

4 The future sons of grief shall sigh,
  While standing round in mystic tie,
And raise their hands, Alas! to heaven,
  In anguish that no hope is given.

5 From whence we come, or whither go,
  Ask me no more, nor seek to know,
Till three shall meet, who formed like them,
  The Grand Lodge of Jerusalem.

        [2*]

55   *Opening. Master Mason.*

1 Great God! wilt thou meet with us here,
  And bless us in our works of love?
Thy sacred name we all revere,
  Oh! grant us blessings from above.

2 May each be found a living stone,
  For heavenly mansions, tried and
    squared;
When all our earthly sands are run,
  The scythe of time find us prepared.

3 By the strong grip of Judah's king,
  May we be raised to realms of peace;
There constant songs of praises sing,
  In that Grand Lodge of endless bliss.

56   *Opening Encampment.*

1 From all that dwell below the skies,
Let the Creator's praise arise.
Let the Redeemer's name be sung
Through every land, by every tongue.

2 Eternal are thy mercies, Lord;
Eternal truth attends thy word:
Thy praise shall sound from shore to shore,
Till suns shall rise and set no more.

57   *Funeral.*

1 Teach us, oh Lord, our days to sum,
  That we to wisdom may incline;
What steps of life are yet to come,
  What gloomy steps of pain and sin!

2 'Tis ours to know that we must die,
  Oh teach us, Lord, how best to live;
Thy love with greater power display,
  Thy grace in larger measure give.

3 One more we yield the ravening tomb,
  'Tis thy command, our Brother dies;
Once more the pall of funeral gloom,
  Once more the tribute of our sighs.

4 Oh teach us, Lord, our days to sum,
  That we to wisdom may incline;
What steps of life are yet to come,
  What gloomy steps of pain and sin!

58   *Doxology.*

Praise God, from whom all blessings flow
Praise him, all creatures here below;
Praise him above, ye heavenly host;
Praise Father, Son, and Holy Ghost.

WELLS. L. M.

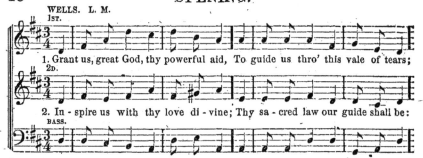

1. Grant us, great God, thy powerful aid, To guide us thro' this vale of tears;

2. In - spire us with thy love di - vine; Thy sa - cred law our guide shall be:

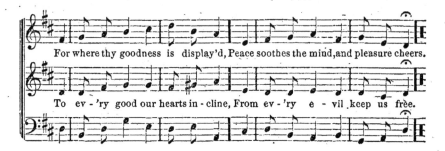

For where thy goodness is display'd, Peace soothes the mind, and pleasure cheers.

To ev - 'ry good our hearts in - cline, From ev - 'ry e - vil keep us free.

60 *Hymn. For Various Occasions.*

1 'Tis Masonry unites mankind,
    To gen'rous actions forms the soul;
In friendly converse all conjoined,
    One spirit animates the whole.

2 Where'er aspiring domes arise,
    Wherever sacred altars stand;
Those altars blaze unto the skies,
    Those domes proclaim the Mason's hand.

3 Sing, brethren, then, the craft we love;—
    Best bond of social joy and mirth;—
Until we meet in Lodge above,
    Proclaim its virtues o'er the earth.

61   *Closing. Royal Arch.*

1 O Lord, behold before thy throne,
    A band of Brothers lowly bend;
Thy face we seek, thy Name we own,
    And pray that thou wilt be our friend.

2 Great God! we come with filial fear,
    To seek a blessing from thy throne;
Our supplications kindly hear,
    Our humble songs be pleased to own.

62   *Opening.*

1 To Thee, O God! to Thee we bring
    The evening's grateful offering;
From thee, the source of joy above,
    Flow everlasting streams of love.

2 Grant us, we pray, a willing mind,
    And how we may thy favor find;
How learn what thou would'st have us do,
    And love and serve each other too.

3 Forgive our sins; our follies hide;
    On earth our wandering footsteps guide;
Subdue our hearts, thy name to love,
    And bring us to thy courts above.

63   *Opening.*

1 Here, gracious God, behold a few,
    Who would observe thy holy Word;
O, may we find thy promise true,—
    That they shall live who fear the Lord.

2 While thus in peace we close the day,
    To every faithful soul be near;
And may we all rejoicing say,
    'Twas good for us to gather here.

64 *Ode for Installation.*

1 Let Masons ever live in love;
Let harmony their blessings prove;
And be the sacred Lodge the place,
Where freedom smiles in every face.

2 Behold the world all in amaze,
Each curious eye with transport gaze;
They look, they like, they wish to be,
What none can gain, except he's free.

3 Let Masons then, with watchful eye,
Regard the works of Charity;
Let Union, Love, and Friendship meet,
And show that Wisdom's ways are sweet.

65 *Ode for Dedication.*

1 Almighty Father! God of Love!
Sacred, eternal King of kings!
From thy celestial courts above,
Send beams of grace on seraph's wings.
O, may they, gilt with light divine,
Shed on our hearts inspiring rays;
While bending at this sacred shrine,
We offer mystic songs of praise.

2 Faith! with divine and heavenward eye,
Pointing to radiant realms of bliss,
Shed here thy sweet benignity,
And crown our works with happiness;
Hope! too, with bosom void of fear,
Still on thy steadfast anchor lean,
O, shed thy balmy influence here,
And fill our breasts with joy serene.

3 And thou, fair Charity! whose smile
Can bid the heart forget its woe,
Whose hand can misery's care beguile,
And kindness' sweetest boon bestow;
Here shed thy sweet, soul-soothing ray;
Soften our hearts, thou Power divine!
Bid the warm gem of pity play,
With sparkling lustre, on our shrine.

4 Thou, who art throned 'midst dazzling light,
And wrapped in brilliant robes of gold,
Whose flowing locks of silvery white
Thy age and honor both unfold:—
Genius of Masonry! descend,
And guide our steps by thy strict law;
O, swiftly to our temple bend,
And fill our breasts with solemn awe.

66 *Sweet is the Memory.*

1 Sweet is the memory of the night,
When first we saw the secret light;
Dear to our souls shall ever be
The mysteries of Masonry.

2 Grateful to thee our hearts we bend,
O Masonry, thou poor man's friend;
Dark though the streams of life may flow,
That still it rolls to thee we owe.

3 O, we have tried thee, tried thee long,
When hope had fled, when hope was str ng,
Brighter than all our fancy dreamed,
Thy true, unfading love has beamed.

4 Science may shoot its bright cold ray
Across the pilgrim's painful way;
Honor may plant the laurel there,
For fortune to usurp and wear:

5 But vain their power to warm, O Art,
The chill, that settles round the heart;
Thou canst alone beguile the hours,
And strew our rugged way with flowers.

67 *Knight Templar.*

1 Rest, holy pilgrim, rest, I pray,
Dreary to Mecca's shrine thy way;
O deign an hermit's hut to share,
Nor proudly spurn his homely fare.

2 But say from whence thy sorrows flow,
Impart each secret source of woe;
For time, I see, and grief have spread
A silver halo o'er thy head.

3 No ruffian lawless steps intrude
To blast the joys of solitude;
But peace and meditation dwell,
Sweet inmates of the hermit's cell.

4 To quench thy thirst the rock shall flow,
To feed thee sweetest fruits shall grow;
Soft dreams shall nature's waste repair,
Then deign an hermit's hut to share.

68 *Royal Arch. Opening.*

1 With all my powers of heart and tongue,
I'll praise my Maker in my song;
Angels shall hear the notes I raise,
Approve the song, and join the praise.

2 I'll sing thy Truth, and Mercy, Lord;
I'll sing the wonders of thy Word;
Not all the works and Names below,
So much thy power and glory show.

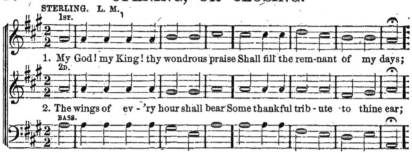

1. My God! my King! thy wondrous praise Shall fill the rem-nant of my days;

2. The wings of ev-'ry hour shall bear Some thankful trib-ute to thine ear;

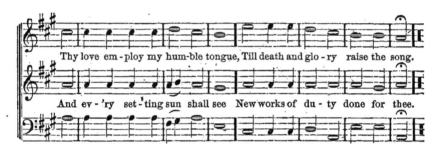

Thy love em-ploy my hum-ble tongue, Till death and glo-ry raise the song.

And ev-'ry set-'ting sun shall see New works of du-ty done for thee.

70　　　*Opening.*

1 Father, we come with filial fear,
　To seek a blessing from thy throne;
Our supplications kindly hear,
　Our humble songs be pleased to own.

2 While here, direct our thoughts aright;
　Let heavenly Truth our minds impress;
When in this temple we unite,
　The hour of worship deign to bless.

71　　　*Opening.*

1 Assembled in this place once more,
　O Lord, thy blessing we implore;
O listen, while we sing and pray,
Be with, and guide us, all our way.

2 Our fervent prayer to thee ascends;
Oh shed thy grace on foes and friends;
And when we in this place appear,
Help us to worship in thy fear.

3 When we on earth shall meet no more,
May we above to glory soar;
And praise thee in more lofty strains,
Where one eternal Sabbath reigns.

72　　　*Closing.*

1 Great God, when from these scenes with-
　　drawn,
　And from thine earthly Sabbaths' light,
May each tried spirit hail the dawn
　Of heaven's eternal Sabbath bright.

2 As one by one we all shall go,
　And leave our places vacant here;
Admit us to that Lodge we know,
　Where never falls the parting tear.

73　　　*Opening, or Closing.*

1 Supreme Grand Master, most sublime,
High throned in glory's radiant clime;
Behold thy sons on bended knee,
Convened, O God, to worship thee.

2 And as 'tis thine, with open ear,
The suppliant voice of prayer to hear;
Grant thou, O Lord, this one request,
Let Masons be, in blessing, blest.

3 O give the craft, from pole to pole,
The feeling heart, the pitying soul —
The generous breast, the lib'ral hand,
Compassion's balm, and mercy's band.

WINDHAM. L. M.

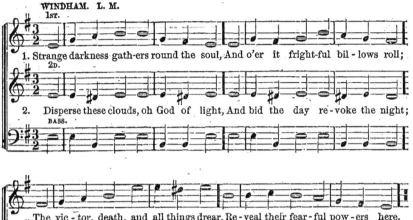

1. Strange darkness gath-ers round the soul, And o'er it fright-ful bil-lows roll;

2. Disperse these clouds, oh God of light, And bid the day re-voke the night;

The vic-tor, death, and all things drear, Re-veal their fear-ful pow-ers here.

Fa-ther of all, ex-tend thy pow'r, And save us in this try-ing hour.

75 *Master Mason.*

1 Dangers of every form attend
    Your steps, as onward you proceed;
No earthly power can now befriend,
  .Or aid you in this time of need.

2 Confide your trust in him alone,
    Who rules all things above, below;
Send your petitions to his throne,
    For he alone can help you now.

76 *Master Mason.*

1 Our life, how short! a groan, a sigh;
  We live — and then begin to die:
But oh! how great a mercy this,
That death's a portal into bliss.

2 My soul! death swallows up thy fears;
The grave shall wipe away all tears;
Why should we fear this parting pain;
We die that we may live again.

77 *Master Mason.*

Unveil thy bosom, faithful tomb,
  .Take this new treasure to thy trust,
And give these sacred relics room
  To slumber in the silent dust.

78 *Super Excellent Master.*

1 When we, our wearied limbs to rest,
    Sat down by proud Euphrates stream,
We wept, with doleful thoughts oppress'd,
    And Zion was our mournful theme.

2 Our harps, that, when with joy we sung,
    Were wont their tuneful parts to bear,
With silent strings, neglected hung,
    On willow trees that withered there.

3 How shall we tune our voice to sing,
    . Or touch our harps with skillful hands?
Shall hymns of joy, to God our King,
    Be sung by slaves in foreign lands?

4 O Salem, our once happy seat!
    When I of thee forgetful prove,
Then let my trembling hand forget
    The tuneful strings with art to move.

5 If I to mention thee forbear,
    Eternal silence seize my tongue;
Or if I sing one cheerful air,
    Till thy deliverance is my song.

HEBRON. L. M.   From "Carmina Sacra," by permission.

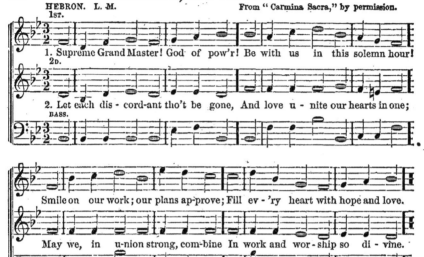

1st.
1. Supreme Grand Master! God of pow'r! Be with us in this solemn hour!

2d.
2. Let each dis - cord-ant tho't be gone, And love u - nite our hearts in one;

BASS.

Smile on our work; our plans ap-prove; Fill ev - 'ry heart with hope and love.

May we, in u-nion strong, com-bine In work and wor - ship so di - vine.

80   *Masonic Hymn.*

1 Grant us, kind Heaven! what we request;
  In Masonry let us be blest:
Direct us to that happy place,
  Where friendship smiles on every face:

2 Where sceptered Reason, from her throne,
  Surveys the Lodge, and makes us one;
And Harmony's delightful sway,
  Forever sheds ambrosial day.

3 No prying eye can view us here,
  No fool or knave disturb our cheer;
Our well-formed laws set mankind free,
  And give relief to misery.

4 Our Lodge the social Virtues grace,
  And Wisdom's rules we fondly trace;
While Nature, open to our view,
  Points out the paths we should pursue.

81   *Charity.*

1 Offspring of heaven! mankind's best friend,
  Bright Charity, inspire our lay;
On these terrestial shores descend,
  And quit the realms of cloudless day.

2 Come, then, all bounteous as thou art,
  And hide thee from our sight no more;
Touch every soul, expand each heart,
  That breathes on freedom's chosen shore.

82   *Relief.*

1 Blest is the man whose tender care,
  Relieves the poor in their distress;
Whose pity wipes the widow's tear,
  Whose hand supports the fatherless.

2 His heart contrives, for their relief,
  More than his willing hands can do:
He, in the time of wasting grief,
  Shall find the Lord his pity too.

3 His soul shall live secure on earth,
  With secret blessings on his head;
When drouth, and pestilence, and dearth,
  Around him multiply their dead.

4 Or, if he languish on his couch,
  God will pronounce his sins forgiven;
Will save him with a healing touch,
  Or take his willing soul to heaven.

83   *Closing.*

1 Spirit of peace, all meek and mild,
  Inspire our hearts, our souls possess;
Repel each passion, rude and wild,
  And bless us as we aim to bless.

2 Hear, now, the parting prayer we pour,
  And bind our hearts in love alone;
Though we may meet on earth no more,
  May we at last surround thy throne.

84   *Knight Templar.*

1 To the Knight Templar's awful dome,
    Where glorious knights in arms are drest,
Filled with surprise, I slowly come,
    With solemn jewels on my breast.

2 A pilgrim to this house I came,
    With sandal, staff, and scrip so white;
Through rugged paths my feet were led;
    All this I bore to be a Knight.

3 With feeble arm I gently smote,
    At the Knight Templar's mercy gate;
What I beheld, when it was op'ed,
    Was splendid, elegant, and great.

4 Twelve dazzling lights I quickly saw,
    All chosen for the cross to fight;
In one of them I found a flaw,
    And speedily put out that light.

5 Unite your hearts, and join your hands
    In every solemn tie of love;
United, each firm Templar stands
    The virtue of his cause to prove.

6 Until the world is lost in fire,
    By order of the Trinity,
The amazing world shall still admire
    Our steadfast love and unity.

85   *Hymn for Consecration.*

1 Master Supreme! accept our praise;
    Still bless this consecrated band;
Parent of Light! illume our ways,
    And guide us by thy sovereign hand.

2 May Faith, Hope, Charity, divine,
    Here hold their undivided reign;
Friendship and Harmony combine
    To soothe our cares, and banish pain.

3 May Wisdom here disciples find,
    Beauty unfold her thousand charms;
Science invigorate the mind,
    Expand the soul, that virtue warms.

4 May Pity dwell within each breast,
    Relief attend the suffering poor;
Thousands by this, our Lodge, be blest,
    Till worth, distrest, shall want no more.

86   *Closing.*

Eternal are thy mercies, Lord;
Eternal truth attends thy word;
Thy praise shall sound from shore to shore,
Till suns shall rise and set no more.

87   *Royal Arch.*

1 Almighty Father! heavenly King!
    Before whose sacred Name we bend,
Accept the praises which we sing,
    And to our humble prayer attend.

2 Thou, who did'st Persia's king command
    A proclamation to extend,
That Israel's host might quit his land,
    Their holy Temple to attend;

3 All hail! great Architect divine!
    Let heaven's eternal arches ring!
This universal frame is thine;
    All hail! thou great, Eternal King!

88   *Opening.*

1 Ye happy few, who here extend
    In peaceful lines, from east to west,
With fervent zeal the Lodge defend,
    And lock its secrets in your breast.

2 Since ye are met upon the Square,
    Bid love and Friendship jointly reign;
Be peace and Harmony your care,
    They form an adamantine chain.

89   *Anniversary Ode.*

1 Hail! sacred art! by Heaven designed
    A gracious blessing for mankind;
Peace, joy, and love, thou dost bestow,
    On us thy votaries below.

2 Bright wisdom's footsteps here we trace,
    From Solomon, the prince of peace,
Whose righteous maxims still we hold
    More precious than rich Ophir's gold.

3 His heavenly proverbs to us tell,
    How we on earth should ever dwell,
In harmony and social love,
    To emulate the blest above.

4 Now, having Wisdom for our guide,
    By its sweet precepts we'll abide;
Nor from its path will ever stray,
    Till all shall meet in endless day.

5 Vain, empty grandeur shall not find
    Its dwelling in a Brother's mind;
A Mason, who is true and wise,
    Its glittering pomp will e'er despise.

6 Candor and friendship, joy and peace,
    Within his breast shall have a place;
Virtue and Wisdom thus combined,
    Shall decorate the Mason's mind.

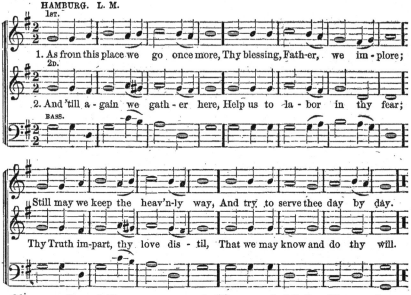

HAMBURG. L. M.
1st.

1. As from this place we go once more, Thy blessing, Fath-er, we im-plore;

2d.

2. And 'till a-gain we gath-er here, Help us to la-bor in thy fear;

BASS.

Still may we keep the heav'n-ly way, And try to serve thee day by day.

Thy Truth im-part, thy love dis - til, That we may know and do thy will.

91　　　*Funeral Hymn.*

1 Here let the sacred rites succeed
    In honor of departed friends;
With solemn order now proceed,
    While living faith with sorrow blends.

2 Now let the hymn—the humble prayer,
    From hearts sincere, ascend on high;
And mystic evergreen declare,
    That Hope within us cannot die.

3 The mortal frame may be concealed
    Within the narrow house of gloom;
But God, in mercy, has revealed
    Immortal life beyond the tomb.

4 The friends we mourn we still may love;
    Then let our aspirations rise,
To that bright spirit-world above,
    Where virtue lives, *love never dies.*

92　　　*Master Mason.*

1 Blest is the man who stands in awe
    Of God, and loves his sacred law;
His seed on earth shall be renowned,
    And with successive honors crowned.

2 Beset with threat'ning dangers round,
    Unmoved shall he maintain his ground;
The sweet remembrance of the just
    Shall flourish, when he sleeps in dust.

93　　　*Installation Ode.*

1 Come all ye gentle springs, that move
    And animate the human mind,
And by your energy improve
    The social bond by which we're joined.

2 This happy Lodge, of care devoid,
    And haggard malice always free,
Shall by your aid be still employed
    In social love and harmony.

3 Oh! let each heart with rapture glow;
    Be every nerve with rapture strung;
May Love from every bosom flow,
    And kindly words from every tongue.

94　　　*Opening.　Red Cross.*

1 "Let there be Light"—the first command
    That burst from heaven's exalted throne!
Jehovah gave the stern decree,
    And forth immediate radiance shone.

2 But there's a light, a brighter light,
    Than sun or nature e'er could claim;
'Tis shed through all creation's space,
    And bears a great and glorious name.

3 Then let us search for this great Light,
    Which shines with such refulgence broad;
Its name is Truth; and that alone
    Can bring our wandering souls to God.

95 *Knight Templar.*

1 The rising God forsakes the tomb;
 Up to his Father's court he flies;
Cherubic legions guard him home,
 And shout him welcome to the skies.

2 Break off your tears, ye saints, and tell
 How high our great deliverer reigns;
Sing how he spoiled the hosts of hell,
 And led the monster, Death, in chains.

3 Say, " live forever glorious King,
 Born to instruct, redeem, and save;"
Then ask—" O Death! where is thy sting?"
 " And where's thy victory?" boasting
 grave!

96 *Master Mason.*

1 Death, like an ever-flowing stream,
Sweeps us away—our life's a dream—
An empty tale—a morning flower—
Cut down and withered in an hour.

2 Teach us, O Lord, how frail is man;
And kindly lengthen out our span,
Till, cleansed by grace, we all may be
Prepared to die, and dwell with thee.

97 *Opening.*

1 O Thou who see'st the sparrow's fall,
 And hear'st the raven's feeble cry,
Whose tender care extends to all,
 To thee we raise the prayerful eye.

2 Father! while we as brothers meet,
 With Truth and Love our bosoms fill,
And 'till we reach our heavenly seat,
 Help us to know and do thy will.

98 *Closing.*

1 Father, once more let grateful praise
 And humble prayer to thee ascend;
Thou Guide and Guardian of our ways,
 Our first and last, and only Friend.

2 Hear, then, the parting prayers we pour,
 And bind our hearts in love alone;
Though we may meet on earth no more,
 May all at last surround thy throne.

99 *Masonic Hymn.*

1 From East to West, o'er land and sea,
 Where brothers meet and friends agree,
Let incense rise from hearts sincere,
 The dearest offering gathered here.

2 Our trust reposed on God alone,
 Who ne'er will contrite hearts disown;
Our faith shall mark that holy light,
 Whose beams our dearest joys unite.

[3]

100 *Royal Arch Hymn.*—F. G. TISDALL.

1 There is a word, no mortal tongue
 May dare its mystic sounds combine;
Nor saint hath breathed, nor prophet sung
 That holiest of the names divine!

2 Nor may the fingers of the Scribe
 Presume that hallowed word to write;
Accursed alike, from Israel's tribe,
 Were he who dared that word indite!

3 Yet though nor lips, nor pen, may dare
 That name unspeakable impart;
'Tis ever breathed in Masons' prayer,—
 'Tis ever written in his heart.

101 *Opening Hymn.*

1 How blest the sacred tie, that binds
 In sweet communion kindred minds!
How swift the heavenly course they run,
 Whose hearts, whose faith, whose hopes
 are one.

2 Together oft they seek the place
 Where Friendship smiles on every face:
How high, how strong their raptures swell
 There's none but kindred souls can tell.

3 Nor shall the glowing flame expire,
 When dimly burns frail nature's fire:
Then shall they meet in realms above —
 A heaven of joy — a heaven of love.

102 *Closing.*

1 We offer, Lord, an humble prayer,
 And thank thee for thy grace bestowed,
In leading us beneath thy care
 Thus far in wisdom's pleasant road.

2 Whatever be our lot may fall,—
 What toilsome duties to fulfil,—
We do not know; but in them all,
 Be thou our strength and comfort still.

3 Be thou, O God, our constant friend —
 Our hope, our comfort, and our stay;
And may thy Spirit, Lord, descend,
 To bless and guide us day by day.

103 *Opening.*

1 O Thou! at whose great Name we bend,
 To whom our warmest vows we pay,
God over all! in love descend,
 And bless the labors of this day.

2 Here, still, through all succeeding time,
 May Truth and Love its tribute bring,
And still the anthem-note sublime,
 To Thee from children's children ring.

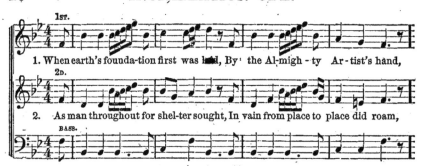

1. When earth's founda-tion first was laid, By the Al-migh-ty Ar-tist's hand,

2. As man throughout for shel-ter sought, In vain from place to place did roam,

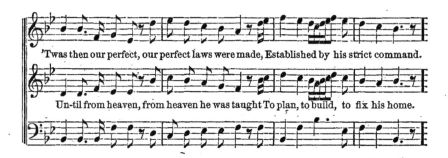

'Twas then our perfect, our perfect laws were made, Established by his strict command.

Un-til from heaven, from heaven he was taught To plan, to build, to fix his home.

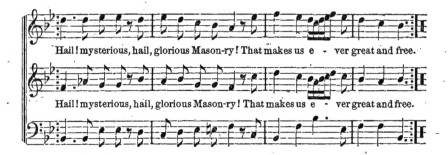

Hail! mysterious, hail, glorious Mason-ry! That makes us e - ver great and free.

Hail! mysterious, hail, glorious Mason-ry! That makes us e - ver great and free.

3 Hence illustrious rosé our Art,
  And now in beauty piles appear,
Which shall to endless, to endless time
    impart,
How worthy and how great we are.
Hail! mysterious, hail, glorious Masonry!
That makes us ever great and free.

4 Nor we less famed for every tie,
  By which the human thought is bound;
Love, truth, and friendship, and sweetest
    unity,
Join all our hearts and hands around.
Hail! mysterious, hail, glorious Masonry!
That makes us ever great and free.

1. Hail! Ma - son - ry, thou craft.... di - vine, Come, breth-ren! let us cheer-ful join, To cel - e-brate this happy day, And homage to our Mas-ter pay.

To cel - e - brate this hap-py day, And hom-age to our Mas-ter.... pay.

2
Hail! happy, blest, and sacred place!
Where friendship brightens every face,
Where mystic art adorns the chair,
Resplendent with his noble square.

3
Come, brethren, cheerful join with me,
To sing the praise of Masonry;
The noble, faithful, and the brave,
Whose art shall live beyond the grave.

28 "WHERE'ER IN THIS WIDE WORLD WE ROVE."

(SHELLS OF OCEAN.) L. M. DOUBLE.   Words by G. W. CHASE.

1. Where'er in this wide world we rove, From North to South, from East to West, We still may

2. Tho' friends forsake, tho' riches fail, And all around seems dark and drear, There still is

share a brother's love, And find relief if sore distress'd, And find relief if sore distress'd. 'Mid Northern

left the mystic hail Whose magic charm our heart can cheer, Whose magic charm our heart can cheer. Oh! happy

cold or Southern heat, On ocean wave or Western wild, A Brother true we still may meet ; By kindly

they who thus can share A Brother's Charity and Love ; And Hoping, Loving, each prepare To dwell at

words our days beguil'd ; A Brother true we still may meet ; By kindly words our days, our days beguil'd

last in Lodge above, And Hoping, Loving, each prepare To dwell at last in Lodge, in Lodge above.

107 *Masonic Song.*—GEO. P. MORRIS.

1 Our Order, like the Ark of Yore,
.Upon the raging seas was tost;
Secure amid the billows' roar
It moved, and nothing has been lost.
When elements discordant seek
To wreck what God in mercy saves,
- The struggle is as vain and weak
As that of the retiring waves.

2 The power who bade the waters cease,—
The pilot of the pilgrim band,—
He gave the gentle dove of peace,
The branch she bore them from the land.
In Him above we put our trust,
With heart and voice, with one accord;
Ascribing with the true and just,
All "Holiness unto the Lord."

- **108** *Dedication of Masonic Hall.*

(BRO. T. J. GREENWOOD, OF DOVER, N. H.)

1 "The Groves were God's first Temples,"
made
That man might early learn to praise,
And bowing in the sylvan shade,
To Thee, O'God, his homage raise.
But *Light* advanced! New Temples sprung
Beneath the craftsman's skilful hand,
That grateful love might find a tongue
Where Wisdom, Strength, and Beauty
. stand.

2 Yet not where Sabbath bells alone
Invite the soul, our God we find,
But where ingenious toil is known,
He deigns to bless th' expanding mind.
This Fane, oh God! our hands have rear'd,
To aid us in our work of love;
And while we've toiled, Thy smile hath
cheered,
Approving from Thy Throne above.

3 We own Thy Light! we plead Thy grace,
To crown our labors day by day,
That this may be a hallowed place,
To speed us on our pilgrim way.
Oh let us wear the triple crown
Of Faith, Hope, Charity divine,
That Thou our humble gift will own,
While Glory, Honor, Praise are Thine.

109 *Opening.*

1 Kind Father, God of love and power,
Be with us at this quiet hour!
Smile on our souls; our plans approve;
Help us to live in peace and love.
Let each discordant thought be gone,
And love unite our hearts in one;
Like brothers true, may we combine
To forward objects so divine.

[3*]

110 *Opening.*

1 Great God, behold before thy throne,
A band of brothers lowly bend;
Thy sacred Name we humbly own,
And pray that thou wilt be our friend.
A band of brothers may we live,
A band of brothers may we die;
To each may God, our Father, give
A home of peace above the sky.

111 *Opening.*

1 Here, gracious God, beneath thy feet,
Again we mystic brothers meet,
Joined by the cord of mutual love,
Bound to our common Friend above.
May Wisdom, Zeal, and Love, inspire
Our bosoms with their purest fire;
While Faith on thine own word relies,
And Hope looks joyful to the skies.

2 Grant us thy presence, God of grace,
Now while we meet before thy face,
That we may feel, ere we depart,
Thy love diffused through every heart.
May Wisdom, Zeal, and Love, inspire
Our bosoms with their purest fire;
While Faith on thine own word relies,
And Hope looks joyful to the skies.

112 *Closing.*

1 As from this place we go once more,
Thy blessing, Father, we implore;
Still may we keep the heavenly way,
And strive to serve thee day by day.
And 'till again we gather here,
Help us to labor in thy fear;
Thy Truth impart, thy love distil,
That we may know and do thy will.

113 *Song.*—JAMES B. TAYLOR, K. T.
Air—" Shells of Ocean."

1 In pensive mood, at close of day,
I seek the peaceful, calm retreat,
Where Truth and Innocence repay
Those brethren dear in Lodge that meet.
The precepts taught by Masons' Art,
To guide and guard our course through
life,
Are grateful to the Virtuous heart,
Suppressing hate—subduing strife.

2 Where brethren meet in solemn form,
Devoted to the Master's will,
To shield from want, or gathering storm,
Their every duty to fulfil:—
In mystic rites we there engage,
And lessons pure and holy learn,
From the unerring, sacred page,
Where Love and Heavenly Truth do
burn.

30 SHOULD AULD ACQUAINTANCE BE FORGOT.

AULD LANG SYNE. C. M.

Words by Bro. ROBERT BURNS.

1. Should auld ac - quain-tance be for - got, And nev - er brought to mind,

2. Then here's a hand, my trus - ty frien', And gie's a hand o' thine,

Should auld ac - quaint-ance be for - got, And days of auld lang syne:

We'll take a right gude wil - lie waught, For auld, for auld lang syne.

For auld lang syne, my dear, For auld lang syne,

For auld - lang syne, my dear, For auld lang syne,

We'll take a cup of kind - ness yet, For auld lang syne.

We'll take a cup of kind - ness yet, For auld lang syne.

Opening Song.—G. W. CHASE.

115

1 Come, Brothers of the plumb and square,
Come, join in cheerful song;
Let every heart and voice prepare
The glad notes to prolong.
We're Brothers, by a mystic tie,
We're Brothers true and Free,
Then let the song ascend on high,—
God speed Freemasonry.

2 In Love we meet, in peace we part;
We walk by plummet's line;-
While Friendship dwells within each heart
That owns the craft Divine.
'Mid all the toils and cares of earth,
We steady keep our way;
With Faith, and Hope, we wait the birth
Of an Eternal day.

116 *Closing Song.*

1 We meet in love, we part in peace,
Our council labors o'er;
We'll ask, ere life's best days shall cease,
To meet in time once more.
CHORUS.
'Mid fairest scenes to memory dear,
In change of joy and pain;
We'll think of friends assembled here,
And hope to meet again.

2 Though changes mark time's onward way
In all we fondly claim,
Fraternal hopes shall ne'er decay —
Our landmarks still the same.
CHORUS.
'Mid fairest scenes to memory dear,
In change of joy and pain;
We'll think of friends assembled here,
And hope to meet again.

3 Our Faith unmoved, with Truth our guide,
As seasons mark our clime;
Through winter's chill, or summer's pride,
We'll hail the Art Sublime.
CHORUS.
'Mid fairest scenes to memory dear,
In change of joy and pain;
We'll think of friends assembled here,
And hope to meet again.

4 When life shall find its silent close,
With Hope's kind promise blest;
In that Grand Lodge may all repose,
Where joys immortal rest.
CHORUS.
'Mid fairest scenes to memory dear,
In change of joy and pain;
We'll think of friends assembled here,
And hope to meet again.

117 *Friendship.*

1 Old friends shall never be forgot,
Whose love was love sincere;
And still, whatever be their lot,
We'll make them welcome here.
The kindness they have often shown,
We long have borne in mind,
And long, we hope, our friends have known,
A welcome where to find.

2 It never shall be said, with truth,
That now our hearts are cold;
The friends who loved us in our youth,
We'll love when they are old.
And if in ills, which we withstand,
They kind assistance need,
We'll stretch them forth a helping hand,
And be a friend indeed.

118 *Closing.*

1 Now we must close our labors here,
Though sad it is to part;
May Love, Relief, and Truth sincere,
Unite each brother's heart.
Now to our homes let's haste away,
Still filled with love and light;
And may each heart in kindness say,
Good night, brother, good night.

119 *Initiation, or Crafting.*

1 O welcome, brother, to our band,
Though strong its numbers now,
And high its lofty pillars stand,
And noble arches bow.
Oh welcome — if thy heart be true,
Thou'lt find with us a home;
We're daily adding columns new
Unto our glorious dome.

2 Now let our ardent prayers arise,
For blessings on his brow,
And bear our offering to the skies,
For him who joins us now.
Oh welcome — if thy heart be true,
Thou'lt find with us a home;
We're daily adding columns new,
Unto our glorious dome.

120 *Closing.*

1 Great Architect of Earth and Heaven,
By time nor space confined,
Enlarge our love to comprehend
Our brethren, all mankind.
With Faith our guide, and humble Hope,
Warm Charity and Love,
May all at last be raised to share
Thy perfect light above.

PETERBORO'. C. M.

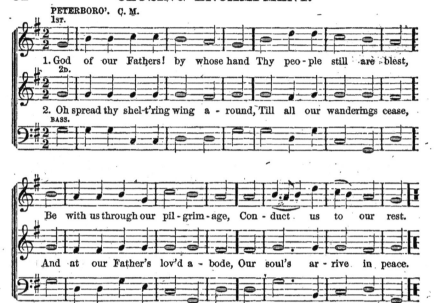

1. God of our Fathers! by whose hand Thy peo-ple still are blest,

2. Oh spread thy shel-t'ring wing a - round, Till all our wanderings cease,

Be with us through our pil - grim - age, Con - duct us to our rest.

And at our Father's lov'd a - bode, Our soul's ar - rive in peace.

122 *Fellow Craft.*

1 May our united hearts expand
    With love's refreshing showers,
Whose warm and kindling glow is felt,
    To cheer our saddest hours.

2 Before our treasured shrine we bow,
    In gratitude sublime;
Imploring still God's saving grace,
    Through all of coming time.

123 *Opening Hymn.*

1 Lo! what an entertaining sight,
    Are brethren who agree;
Brethren, whose cheerful hearts unite
    In bonds of piety.

2 'Tis like the oil, divinely sweet,
    On Aaron's reverend head;
The trickling drops perfumed his feet,
    And o'er his garments spread.

3 'Tis pleasant as the morning dews,
    That fell on Zion's hill;
Where God his mildest glory shows,
    And makes his grace distil.

124 *Encampment.*

Let God — the Father and the Son
    And Spirit, be adored,
Where there are works to make him known,
    Or saints to love the Lord.

125 *Master Mason. Opening.*

1 Almighty Father! gracious Lord!
    Kind Guardian of our days!
Thy mercies let our hearts record,
    In songs of grateful praise.

2 Lord, when this mortal frame decays,
    And every weakness dies,
Complete the wonders of thy grace,
    And raise us to the skies.

126 *The Lord's Prayer.*

1 Our Father, who in heaven art!
    All hallowed be thy Name;
Thy kingdom come, thy will be done,
    Throughout this earthly frame,—

2 As cheerfully as 'tis by those
    Who dwell with Thee on high:
Lord, let thy bounty, day by day,
    Our daily food supply.

3 As we forgive our enemies,
    Thy pardon, Lord, we crave;
Into temptation lead us not,
    But us from evil save.

4 For kingdom, power, and glory, all
    Belong, O Lord, to thee;
Thine from eternity they were,
    And thine shall ever be.

139 *Royal Arch.*

1. How precious is the book divine,
   That unto us is given;
   Bright as a lamp its doctrines shine,
   To guide our souls to heaven.

2. It sweetly cheers our drooping hearts,
   In this dark vale of tears;
   Life, light, and joy it still imparts,
   And quells our rising fears.

3. This lamp, through all the tedious night
   Of life, shall guide our way;
   Till we behold the clearer light
   Of an eternal day.

140 *Opening.*

1. Lo! what an entertaining sight
   Those friendly brethren prove,
   Whose cheerful hearts in bands unite,
   Of harmony and love!

2. 'Tis pleasant as the morning dews
   That fall on Zion's hill,
   Where God his radiant glory shows,
   And makes his grace distil.

141 *Opening.*

1. Oh, influence sweet, from spheres above
   This rude and selfish life,
   Descend and dwell with us in love,
   Dispelling scenes of strife.

2. Let darkness spread no more its wings
   With passion's brooding powers,
   Where love and wisdom e'er should reign
   In this retreat of ours.

3. Oh, influence sweet, from spheres above,
   Surround, and make us good,
   And ever let us feel we have
   A loving Brotherhood.

142 *Mark Master.*

1. How sweet, how calm this Sabbath morn,
   How pure the air that breathes,
   And soft the sounds upon it borne,
   And light its vapor wreaths!

2. Let each unholy passion cease,
   Each evil thought be crushed,
   Each anxious care that mars our peace
   In Faith and Love be hushed.

143 *Fellow-Craft. Work.*

1. O welcome, brother, to our band,
   Though strong its numbers now,
   And high its lofty pillars stand,
   And noble arches bow.

2. O welcome — if thy heart be true,
   Thou'lt find with us a home;
   We're daily adding columns new
   Unto our glorious dome.

3. Now let our heartfelt prayers arise,
   For blessings on his brow,
   And bear our offering to the skies,
   For him who joins us now.

144 *Master Mason. Opening.*

1. Come, Masters of the Art, unite,
   And may this meeting prove,
   To all th' assembled sons of light,
   A strengthened bond of love.

2. May Friendship and Morality,
   With true fraternal love,
   Be found in every Mason's heart,
   And all his actions move.

145 *Opening, or Closing.*

1. To thee we look, thou Power supreme!
   Thou wilt our wants supply!
   Safe in thy presence shall we live,
   And in thy favor die.

2. From thee our vital breath we drew;
   Our childhood was thy care;
   And vigorous youth and feeble age
   Thy kind protection share.

3. Then be it ours, through gentle deeds
   Of pure and perfect love,
   To sow in human hearts the seeds
   Of flowers that bloom above.

146 *Opening, or Closing.*

1. Sweet as the dew on herb and flower,
   That silently distils,
   At evening's soft and balmy hour,
   On Zion's fruitful hills.

2. So, with mild influence from above,
   Shall promised grace descend;
   Till universal peace and love
   O'er all the earth extend.

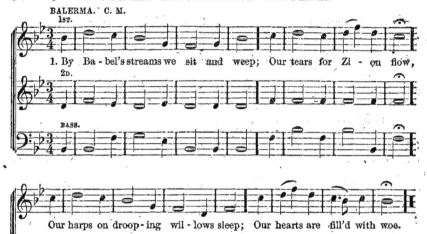

BALERMA. C. M.

1. By Ba-bel's streams we sit and weep; Our tears for Zi - on flow,

Our harps on droop-ing wil-lows sleep; Our hearts are fill'd with woe.

147   *Super Excellent Master.*

1 By Babel's streams we sit and weep;
  Our tears for Zion flow;
Our harps on drooping willows sleep;
  Our hearts are filled with woe.

(SQUARE.)

2 Our walls no more resound with praise;
  Our Temple, foes destroy;
Judea's courts no more upraise
  Triumphant songs of joy.

(TRIANGLE.)

3 Here, mourning, toiling, captive bands,
  Our feasts and Sabbaths cease;
Our tribes dispersed through distant lands,
  And hopeless of release.

(CIRCLE.)

4 But should the ever-gracious Power,
  To us propitious be;
Chaldeans shall our race restore,
  And Kings proclaim us free!

148   *Closing. Royal Arch.*

1 Great God! our King! to thee we raise
  Our voice and all our powers;
Unwearied songs of grateful praise
  Shall fill the circling hour.

2 Thy Name shall dwell upon our tongue
  While suns shall set and rise,
And tune our everlasting song
  When time and nature dies.

149   *Anniversary Hymn.*

1 To Him who rules, be homage paid,
  Where hearts with voice unite;
To him we bring fraternal aid,
  Who guides in solemn rite.

2 Come, Brothers, bound by kindly ties,
  Your notes harmonious bring;
While acts of generous sacrifice,
  In thoughts of love we sing.

3 As days and years roll silent by—
  As Time's sad changes rise,
No doubt shall dim the trusting eye,
  Where rule the good and wise.

4 To Him who rules, be homage paid,
  Where hearts with voice unite;
Till life shall cease, and time shall fade,
  We'll bring our solemn plight.

150 *Encampment.*

1 How glorious is the gift of Faith, .
That cheers the darksome tomb,
And through the damp and gloomy grave
Can shed a rich perfume!

2 Triumphant Faith! it lifts the soul
Above desponding fear;
Exults in hope of heaven, her home,
And longs to enter there!

151 *Funeral Hymn.*

1 Another hand is beckoning us,
Another call is given;
And glows once more, with angel steps,
The path that leads to heaven.

2 Dust, to its narrow house beneath!
Soul, to its place on high!
They that have seen thy look in death,
No more may fear to die.

3 Lone are the paths, and sad the bowers,
Whence thy meek smile is gone;
But, oh! a brighter home than ours,
In heaven, is now thine own.

152 *Master Mason.*

1 The Lord unto thy prayer attend,
In trouble's darksome hour:
The name of Jacob's God defend,
And shield thee by his power.

2 Should friends and kindred, near and dear,
Leave thee to want, or die,
May Heaven make thy life its care,
And all thy need supply.

153 *Funeral Hymn.*

1 As distant lands beyond the sea,
When friends go thence, draw nigh;
So heaven, when friends have thither gone,
Draws nearer from the sky.

2 And as those lands the dearer grow,
When friends are long away,
So heaven itself, through loved ones dead,
Grows dearer day by day.

3 Heaven is not far from those who see
With the pure spirit's sight,
But near, and in the very hearts
Of those who see aright.

[4]

154 *Master Mason.*

1 Few are thy days, and full of woe,
O man, of woman born!
Thy doom is written, "Dust thou art,
And shalt to dust return."

2 Determined are the days that fly
Successive o'er thy head;
The numbered hour is on the wing,
Which lays thee with the dead.

155 *Opening.*

1 Father of all! in every age,
In every clime adored,
By saint, by savage, or by sage,
The universal Lord.

2 To thee, whose temple is all space,
Whose altar, earth, sea, skies,
One chorus let all beings raise,
All nature's incense rise

156 *Master Mason.*

1 Teach me the measure of my days,
Thou maker of my frame;
I would survey life's narrow space,
And learn how frail I am.

2 A span is all that we can boast,
How short the fleeting time!
Man is but vanity and dust,
In all his flower and prime.

157 *Anniversary Ode.*

1 All hail! the great mysterious Art,
Grand offering from above —
Which fondly twines each genial heart
In harmony and love.

2 Come, Brothers, join the festive board,
Awake the tuneful lay;
Unite in Friendship, Peace, and Love;
'Tis Masons' holyday.

3 Come, bring the wreath, the trio bind ·—
Faith, Charity, and Love;
To great St. John a splendid star
In the Grand Lodge above.

4 With fervent Zeal and pure delight,
We'll wake the joyful strain,
Till in the great Grand Lodge we meet,
Where joys immortal reign.

158   *Opening Encampment.*

1 Joy to the world, the Lord is come;
. Let earth receive her King:
Let every heart prepare him room,
    And heav'n and nature sing.

2 Joy to the earth,—the Saviour reigns;
Let men their songs employ;
While fields and floods, rocks, hills and
    plains,
Repeat the sounding joy.

4 He rules the world with truth and grace,
    And makes the nations prove
The glories of his righteousness,
    And wonders of his love.

159   *Anniversary Ode.*

1 Jehovah, God! thy gracious power
    On every hand we see;
O may the blessings of each hour
    Lead all our thoughts to thee.

2 From morn till noon, till latest eve,
    The hand of heaven we see;
And all the blessings we receive
    Proceed direct from thee.

3 In all the varying scenes of time,
    On thee our hopes depend;
Through every age, in every clime,
    Our Father and our Friend!

160 *Royal Arch.*

1 When orient Wisdom beamed serene,
And pillar'd Strength arose;
When Beauty tinged the glowing scene,
And Faith her mansion chose;

2 Exulting bands the fabric viewed,
Mysterious powers adored;
And high the Triple Union stood,
That gave the *Mystic Word.*

3 Pale Envy withered at the sight,
And, frowning at the pile,
Called Murder from the realms of night,
To blast the glorious toil;

4 With ruffian outrage, joined in woe,
They form the league abhorred,
And wounded Science felt the blow
That crushed the *Mystic Word.*

5 At length through time's expanded sphere,
Fair Science spreads her way,
And warmed by Truth's refulgence clear,
Reflects the kindred ray;

6 A second fabric's towering height
Proclaims the *sign* restored,
From whose foundation, brought to light,
Is drawn the *Mystic Word.*

161 *Opening.*

1 Within our temple, met again,
With hearts and purpose strong,
We'll raise our notes of grateful praise,
With union in our song.

2 Around our altar's sacred shrine,
May Love's pure incense rise,
Bearing upon its mystic flame
Our music to the skies.

162 *God, the Creator.*

1 Eternal Wisdom, thee we praise,
Thee all thy creatures sing;
While with thy name, rocks, hills, and seas,
And heaven's high arches ring.

2 Almighty power and equal skill
Shine through the worlds abroad;
Our souls with vast amazement fill,
And speak the Builder — God.

163 *Charity.*

1 O Charity! thou heavenly grace,
All tender, soft and kind;
A friend to all the human race,
To all that's good and kind.

2 The man of charity extends
To all his liberal hand;
His kindred, neighbors, foes and friends,
His pity may command.

3 He aids the poor in their distress —
He hears when they complain;
With tender heart delights to bless,
And lessen all their pain.

4 The sick, the prisoner, poor and blind,
And all the sons of grief,
In him a benefactor find;
He loves to give relief.

5 Oh! may we all in love abound,
And Charity pursue;
Thus shall we be with glory crowned,
And love as angels do.

164 *The Good Samaritan.*

1 Blest is the man whose generous heart
Feels all another's pain;
To whom the supplicating eye
Is never raised in vain; —

2 Whose breast expands with gen'rous warmth,
A brother's woes to feel,
And bleeds in pity o'er the wound
He wants the power to heal.

3 He spreads his kind supporting arms
To every child of grief;
His secret bounty largely flows,
And brings unasked relief.

4 To gentle offices of love
His feet are never slow;
He views, through Mercy's melting eye,
A Brother in a foe.

5 To him protection shall be shown;
And mercy from above
Descend on those, who thus fulfil
The perfect law of love.

CORONATION. C. M.

Bring forth the roy - al di - a - dem, And crown him Lord of all.

165   *Knights Templar.*

1 All hail! the great Immanuel's name!
    Let angels prostrate fall;
   Bring forth the royal diadem,
    And crown him Lord of all.

2 Let every kindred, every tribe,
    On this terrestial ball,
   To him all majesty ascribe,
    And crown him Lord of all.

3 Oh! that with yonder sacred throng,
    We at his feet may fall;
   And join the everlasting song,
    And crown him Lord of all.

166   *The Book of the Law.*

1 How precious is the book divine,
    By inspiration given;
   Bright as a lamp its doctrines shine,
    To guide our souls to heaven.

2 It sweetly cheers our drooping hearts,
    In this dark vale of tears,
   Life, light, and joy it still imparts,
    And quells our rising fears.

3 This lamp, through all the tedious night
    Of life, shall guide our ways;
   Till we behold the clearer light
    Of an Eternal Day.

DUNDEE. C. M.
1st.

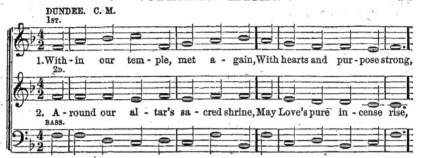

1. With - in   our   tem - ple, met   a - gain, With hearts and pur - pose strong,

2D.

2. A - round our   al - tar's sa - cred shrine, May Love's pure in - cense rise,

BASS.

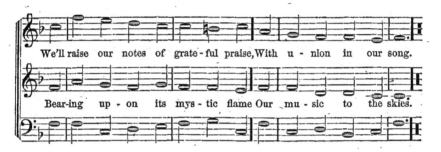

We'll raise   our   notes of grate - ful praise, With u - nion   in   our song.

Bear-ing   up - on   its mys - tic flame Our mu - sic   to   the skies.

168   *Opening.*

1 While thee we seek, protecting Power!
  Be our vain wishes stilled;
And may this consecrated hour,
  With better hopes be filled.

2 In all the varying scenes of time,
  On thee our hopes depend;
Through every age, in every clime,
  Our Father and our Friend.

169   *All Men are Equal.*

1 All men are equal in their birth,
  Heirs of the earth and skies;
All men are equal, when that earth
  Fades from their dying eyes.

2 All wait alike on him, whose power
  Upholds the life he gave;
The Sage, within his star-lit tower,
  The savage in his cave.

3 Ye great! renounce your earthborn pride;
  Ye low! your shame and fear;
And, as ye worship, side by side,
  Your common claims revere.

     [4*]

170   *Opening, or Closing.*

1 Jehovah, God! thy gracious power
  On every hand we see;
O may the blessings of each hour
  Lead all our thoughts to thee.

2 O may we all in love abound,
  And Charity pursue;
Thus shall we be with glory crowned,
  And love as angels do.

171   *Royal Arch. Opening.*

1 Holy and reverend is thy Name,
  Oh thou eternal King!
"Thrice holy Lord," the angels cry,
  "Thrice holy," let us sing!

2 With sacred awe pronounce his Name,
  Whom words nor thoughts can reach;
A holy heart shall please him more
  Than noblest forms of speech.

172   *Closing.*

1 Through endless years, thou art the same,
  O thou eternal God!
Ages to come shall know thy name,
  And tell thy works abroad.

LANESBORO. C. M.
1ST.

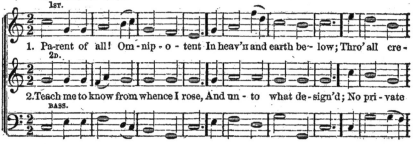

1. Pa-rent of all! Om-nip-o-tent In heav'n and earth be-low; Thro' all cre-

2D.

2.Teach me to know from whence I rose, And un-to what de-sign'd; No pri-vate

BASS.

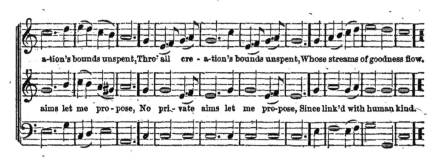

a-tion's bounds unspent, Thro' all cre-a-tion's bounds unspent, Whose streams of goodness flow.

aims let me pro-pose, No pri-vate aims let me pro-pose, Since link'd with human kind.

3 But chief to hear fair virtue's voice,
    May all my thoughts incline;
  'Tis reason's law, 'tis wisdom's choice,
    'Tis nature's call and thine.

4 We from our sacred order's cause,
    Let nothing e'er divide;
  Grandeur, nor gold, nor vain applause,
    Nor friendship false misguide.

5 Teach me to feel a brother's grief,
    To do in all what's best;
  To suffering man give kind relief,
    And blessing to be blest.

174   *Initiation.*

1 Spirit of power and might! behold
    Thy willing servant here;
  With thy protection him infold,
    And free his heart from fear.

2 Tho' darksome skies shall o'er him lower,
    And dangers fill the way;
  Support him with thy gracious power,
    And be his constant stay.

175   *Opening, or Anniversary.*

1 Behold! how pleasant and how good,
    For brethren, such as we
  Of the accepted brotherhood,
    To dwell in unity.

2 'Tis like the oil on Aaron's head,
    Which to his feet distils;
  Like Hermon's dew, so richly shed
    On Zion's sacred hills.

3 For there the Lord of light and love
    A blessing sent with power;
  Oh, may we all this blessing prove,
    E'en life forevermore.

4 On Friendship's altar, rising here,
    Our hands now plighted be,—
  To live in *love* with hearts sincere,
    In *peace* and *unity.*

176   *Closing Encampment.*

Let God, the Father and the Son
    And Spirit be adored,
Where there are works to make him known,
    Or saints to love the Lord.

CHINA. C. M.

1. Why do we mourn de-part-ing friends, Or shake at death's a-larms?

2. Are we not tend-ing up-ward too, To heavn's de-sir'd a-bode?

'Tis but the voice the Fa-ther sends, To call them to his arms.

Why should we wish the hours more slow, Which keep us from our God.

178 *Closing.*

1 Now we must close our labors here,
  Though sad it is to part;
May *Love, Relief,* and *Truth* sincere,
  Unite each brother's heart.

2 Now to our homes we haste away,
  Still filled with love and light;
And may each heart in kindness say,
  Good night, brother, good night.

179 *Opening.*

1 Within our temple met again,
  With hearts and purpose strong,
We'll raise our notes of grateful praise,
  With Union in our song.

2 Around our altar's sacred shrine,
  May Love's pure incense rise,
Bearing upon its mystic flame
  Our music to the skies.

180 *Master Mason.*

Life is a span — a fleeting hour —
  How soon the vapor flies!
Man is a tender, transient flower,
  That e'en in blooming — dies.

181 *Funeral Hymn.*

1 Slowly, in sadness and in tears,
  We leave his dwelling now;
It came not once within our fears,
  He could so early go.

2 We loved to think of him as one
  To whom long years were given;
Who much of good would yet have done,
  And late return to heaven.

3 Fair rose his sun of life — few such —
  Alas! it set at noon;
His Master must have loved him much,
  To call him home so soon.

4 Slowly, in sadness and in tears,
  We'll pass his dwelling by;
We mourn the shortness of his years,
  And bless his memory.

182 *Master Mason.*

Few are thy days, and full of woe,
  O man, of woman born!
Thy doom is written, "dust thou art,
  And shall to dust return."

44 COME, LET US JOIN IN CHEERFUL SONG.

FRENCH AIR. C. M.   Words by G. W. CHASE.

1. Come, let us join in cheerful song, Our voi-ces sounding free;

CHORUS. Then let us join in cheerful song, Our voi-ces sounding free;

In joy-ful notes a-loud pro-long The praise of Ma-son-ry.

Let ev-'ry voice u-nite and sing The cho-rus loud and free,

And ev-'ry heart just tri-bute bring, From mountain, land and sea.

2 Come great and small, come old and young,
  Come all ye Accepted Free;
Come every nation, every tongue,
  And sing of Masonry.
Let Jew nor Gentile e'er forget
  Our honors they may claim;
We're Brothers, on the *level* met,
  Whate'er our land or name.
    Then let us join, &c.

3 Let trusting Faith, and holy Hope,
  And heaven-born Charity,
In every heart have largest scope,
  And shine for Masonry:
Let Justice *circle*, Virtue *square;*
  Let Friendship guide our feet,
So that at last, like jewels rare,
  We all in heaven may meet.
    Then let us join, &c.

184 *Opening Song.*—G. W. CHASE.

1 Come, Brothers of the plumb and square,
  Come, join in cheerful song;
Let every heart and voice prepare
  The glad notes to prolong.
We're Brothers, by a mystic tie,
  We're Brothers true and Free,
Then let the song ascend on high,—
  God speed Freemasonry.
    Then, Brothers of the plumb, &c.

2 In Love we meet, in peace we part;
  We walk by plummet's line;
While Friendship dwells within each heart
  That owns the craft Divine.
'Mid all the toils and cares of earth,
  We steady keep our way;
With Faith, and Hope, we wait the birth
  Of an Eternal day.
    Then, Brothers of the plumb, &c.

185 *Closing Song.*

1 We met in love, we part in peace,
  Our council labors o'er;
We'll ask, ere life's best days shall cease,
  To meet in time once more.
'Mid fairest scenes to memory dear,
  In change of joy and pain;
We'll think of friends assembled here,
  And hope to meet again.
    We met in love, &c.

2 Though changes mark time's onward way
  In all we fondly claim,
Fraternal hopes shall ne'er decay —
  Our landmarks still the same.
Our Faith unmoved, with Truth our guide,
  As seasons mark our clime;
Through winter's chill, or summer's pride,
  We'll hail the Art Sublime.
    We met in love, &c.

186 *Song of the World.*

1 This world is not so bad a world
  As some would like to make it:
Though whether good, or whether bad,
  Depends on how you take it;
For if we scold and fret all day,
  From dewy morn till even,
This world will ne'er afford to man
  A foretaste here of heaven.
    This world is not, &c.

2 This world in truth's as good a world,
  As e'er was known to any
Who have not seen another yet,
  And there are very many;
And if the men, and women too,
  Have plenty of employment,
They surely must be hard to please,
  Who cannot find enjoyment.
    This world is not, &c.

3 This world is quite a pleasant world,
  In rain or pleasant weather;
If people would but learn to live
  In harmony together;
And cease to burst the kindling bond,
  By love and peace cemented,
And learn that best of lessons yet,
  To always be contented.
    This world is not, &c.

4 Then were this world a pleasant world,
  And pleasant folks were in it,
The day would pass most pleasantly,
  To those who thus begin it;
And all the nameless grievances
  Brought on by borrowed troubles,
Would prove, as certainly they are,
  A mass of empty bubbles.
    This world is not, &c.

187

1 Let Masonry, from pole to pole,
  Her sacred laws expand;
Far as the mighty waters roll,
  To wash remotest land;
That virtue has not left mankind,
  Her social maxims prove;
For stamped upon the Mason's mind,
  Are unity and love.
    Let Masonry, &c.

2 Ascending to her native sky,
  Let Masonry increase;
A glorious pillar raised on high,
  Integrity its base.
Peace adds to olive boughs entwined
  An emblematic dove,
As stamped upon the Mason's mind,
  Is unity and love.
    Let Masonry, &c.

CLOSING HYMN.

JERUSALEM. C. M. DOUBLE.

1. Al - migh-ty Fa-ther! heav'nly King! Who rul'st the worlds a - bove;

2. O give us wis - dom from a - bove, Life's va - rious scenes to meet;

Help us our clos-ing hymn to sing With grat - i - tude and love.

Let thy right hand di - rect our way, And guide each brother's feet.

Long may we live in U - nion here, In bonds of so - cial bliss;

And when be - fore Thee we ap - pear, In our e - ter - nal home,

And ma - ny years, our hearts to cheer, Re - turn sweet scenes like this.

May faith-ful hearts still wor - ship here, And praise Thee in our room.

189 *Song for the twenty-fourth of June.*

(BRO. C. MOORE, ED. OF MASONIC REVIEW.)

1 All hail! the twenty-fourth of June,
    Another year has flown,
And on our altar glimmers yet
    The Light which long has shone.
Our brethren! ye are welcome here—
    A truthful—noble band;
We're one in mystic bonds to-day,
    We're one in heart and hand.

2 On this, another festive day,
    We meet as oft of yore,
And tell of mystic labors done
    On mountain, vale, and shore:
Of future work we yet may do,
    Ere we are gathered home,
To hear from our Great Master's lips
    The welcome words—" well done."

3 How sad the thought on memory's page,
    That some who once were here,
Have no place now but in our hearts—
    They've reached a higher sphere:
But Hope points on to future years,
    When, all our works complete,
The true, and tried, and loved of earth,
    Together *all* shall meet.

4 Then hail the twenty-fourth of June!
    Its memories all are dear;
And oft on festive days like this,
    Through many a passing year,
We'll meet and grasp each other's hands,
    Ere yet our work is done,
And, round our altars, closer draw
    The bonds which make us one.

190 *Brotherly Love.*

1 How sweet, how heavenly is the sight,
    When those that love the Lord,
In one another's peace delight,
    And thus fulfil his word!
When each can feel his brother's sigh,
    And with him bear a part;
When sorrow flows from eye to eye,
    And joy from heart to heart.

2 When, free from envy, scorn, and pride,
    Our wishes all above,
Each can his brother's failings hide,
    And show a brother's love!
Love is the golden chain that binds
    The happy souls above;
And he's an heir of heaven that finds
    His bosom glow with love.

191 *The American Freemason.*

BY BRO. ROB. MORRIS.

1 Oh what a goodly heritage
    The Lord to us hath given!
How blest the Brothers here that pledge
    Their Mason vows to heaven!
I sing the mystic chain that binds
    These Western realms in one,—
Such loving hearts, such liberal minds,
    No other land has known.

2 Four thousand Lights, in Mason's halls,
    Are gleaming on our eyes;
Four thousand emblems on our walls
    Tell *whence* that gleaming is;
And when the portals move to pass
    The humble seeker in,
The voice of prayer pervades the place,
    And proves the Light DIVINE.

3 On every hill our dead they lie,
    And green sprigs deck the knoll;
Their fall was moisture to the eye,
    But triumph to the soul.
Our orphans smile in every home,
    Our widow's hearts are glad;
Our "Light" dispels the darkest gloom,
    And comfort finds the sad.

4 Thus link in link, from shore to shore,
    The mystic chain is bound;
Oh, blended thus forevermore
    May Masons' hearts be found:
And while the heavens, on pillars sure
    Of Strength and Wisdom stand,
May Brotherhood like ours endure,
    Where Strength and Wisdom blend.

192 *Opening Hymn.*

1 O God! we lift our hearts to thee,
    And grateful voices raise;
We thank thee for this festive night,—
    Accept our humble praise.
Here may our souls delight to bless
    The God of truth and grace,
Who crowns our labors with success,
    Among the rising race!

2 May each unholy passion cease,
    Each evil thought be crushed,
Each anxious care that mars our peace
    In Faith and Love be hushed.
Oh! may we all in Truth abound,
    And Charity pursue;
Thus shall we be with glory crowned,
    And love as angels do.

Moderato. C. M.
1st.

1. Let Ma - son-ry from pole to pole Her sacred laws ex-pand, Far as the mighty

2d.

2. As-cend-ing to her na - tive sky, Let Ma-son-ry in - crease; A glo-rious pil-lar

BASS.

3

wa - ters roll, To wash re-mo-test land.......... To wash re - motest land: That

rais'd on high, In - teg - ri - ty its base,......... In - teg - ri - ty its base. Peace

vir - tue has not left man-kind, Her so-cial maxims prove, For stamp'd upon the

adds to ol - ive boughs entwin'd, An em-ble-mat-ic dove, As stamp'd upon the

Mason's mind, Are u - ni - ty and love, Are u - ni - ty and love.

Mason's mind, Is u - ni - ty and love, Is u - ni - ty and - love.

"THE INGLE SIDE." C. M.   Words by G. W. CHASE.

1. As morn-ing breeze in balm-y spring, Or sum-mer's gen-tle show'r; As
2. 'Tis there we feel the joys that rise In each true Ma-son's heart, As
3. There Faith, and Hope, and Char-i-ty, In bright-est col-ors shine, While

joy-ous notes the May birds bring, Or per-fume of wild flow'r; So
in the scenes of life he tries To act a Broth-er's part,— 'Tis
Truth, and Love, and U-ni-ty, Pro-claim our Art Di-vine. There

sweet to me the qui-et eve, I met with such as you, And
there the heart may speak its joy, Its trou-ble and its fear; No
Friendship smiles on ev-'ry face, For such as you and me; Oh!

round the al-tar vow to cleave To ev-'ry Bro-ther true.
cow-an near, that can an-noy, No dull, un-friend-ly ear.
may I ev-er find a place A-mong th' Ac-cept-ed Free.

[5]

SILVER ST. S. M.

1. Come, sound his praise a - broad, And hymns of glo - ry sing:

2. Come, wor - ship at his throne, Come, bow be - fore the Lord;

Je - ho - vah is the sov - 'reign God, The u - ni - ver - sal King.

We are his work, and not our own: He form'd us by his word.

196   *Opening.*

1 Blest are the sons of peace,
   Whose hearts and hopes are one;
  Whose kind designs to serve and please,
   Through all their actions run.

2 Blest is this happy place,
   Where Zeal and friendship meet;
  Where Truth, and Love, and heav'nly grace,
  Make our communion sweet.

3 Thus on the heavenly hills
   May we be blest above;
  Where joy, like morning dew, distils,
  And all the air is love.

197   *Royal Arch. Opening.*

1 Thy Name, almighty Lord!
   Shall sound through distant lands;
  Great is thy grace, and sure thy Word;
  Thy Truth forever stands.

2 Far be thine honor spread,
   And long thy praise endure,
  Till morning light and evening shade
  Shall be exchanged no more.

198   *Dedication, &c.*

1 Blest be the tie that binds
   Our hearts in virtuous love:
  The fellowship of kindred minds,
  Is like to that above.

2 Before our Father's throne,
   We pour our ardent prayers;
  Our fears, our hopes, our aims are one,
  Our comforts and our cares.

3 When we asunder part,
   It gives us inward pain:
  But we shall still be joined in heart,
  And hope to meet again.

4 This glorious hope revives
   Our courage by the way;
  While each in expectation lives,
  And longs to see the day.

5 From sorrow, toil and pain,
   And sin, we shall be free;
  And perfect love and friendship reign
  Through all eternity.

ST. THOMAS. S. M.

1. My soul, re - peat his praise, Whose mer-cies are so great;
1. High as the heav'ns are rais'd A - bove the ground we tread;

Whose an - ger is so slow to rise, So rea-dy to a - bate.
So far the rich - es of his grace Our high - est thoughts ex - ceed.

200   *Opening, or Closing.*

1 Great source of light and love,
  To thee our songs we raise!
Oh in the temple, Lord, above,
  Hear and accept our praise!

2 May this fraternal band,
  In Faith and Hope be blessed;
In Charity thrice blessed stand,
  In purity be dressed.

3 May all the sons of peace
  Their every grace improve,
'Till discord through the nations cease,
  And all the world be love.

201   *Opening Encampment.*

1 Let songs of endless praise
  From every heart arise;
Let all the lands their tribute raise,
  To God, who rules the skies.

2 His mercy and his love
  Are boundless as his name;
And all eternity shall prove
  His Truth remains the same.

202   *Royal Arch. Closing.*

1 Companions, we have met,
  And passed a peaceful hour;
These moments may we ne'er forget,
  But hope and pray for more.

2 Through this, and every night,
  Lord, grant us sweet repose;
Now aid us, by thy holy light,
  This Royal Arch to close.

203   *Closing.*

1 Now brothers we must part,
  Where we have met in peace;
Where harmony its joys impart,
  And strife and discord cease.

2 We on the Level meet,
  Upon the Square we part;
May truth, and love, and friendship sweet,
  Pervade each brother's heart.

3 Here, Lord, before we part,
  Help us to bless thy name;
Let every tongue, and every heart,
  Praise and adore the same.

OLMUTZ. S. M.

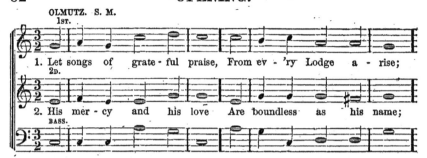

1. Let songs of grate-ful praise, From ev-'ry Lodge a-rise;
2. His mer-cy and his love Are boundless as his name;

Let ev-'ry heart its **tri**-bute raise To God, who rules the skies.

And all e-ter-ni-ty shall prove His truth re-mains the same.

205   *Closing.*

1 Now brothers we must part,
  Where we have met in peace;
Where harmony its joys impart,
And strife and discord cease.

2 We on the Level meet,
  Upon the Square we part;
May Truth, and love, and friendship sweet,
Pervade each brother's heart.

3 Here, Lord, before we part,
  Help us to bless thy name;
Let every tongue, and every heart,
Praise and adore the same.

206   *Royal Arch. Closing.*

1 Companions, we have met
  And passed a peaceful hour;
These moments may we ne'er forget,
But hope and pray for more.

2 Through this, and every night,
  Lord, grant us sweet repose;
Now aid us, by thy holy light,
This Royal Arch to close.

207   *Funeral Hymn.*

1 Come, brethren of the craft,
  Come shed a tear of grief
For our beloved friend, bereft
Of life—a sad relief.

2 Kind Heaven! let angels wing
  Their way to earth again,
And waft a soul—the guest we bring,
To bliss, e'er to remain.

3 Let us, the grave behold!
  And lift our thoughts above;
And mourn our loss, as yet untold,
And raise him still in love.

208   *Encampment. Closing.*

1 Once more, before we part,
  O bless the Saviour's name;
Let every tongue and every heart
Praise and adore the same.

2 Lord, in thy grace we came;
  That blessing still impart;
We met in Jesus' sacred name,
In his dear name we part.

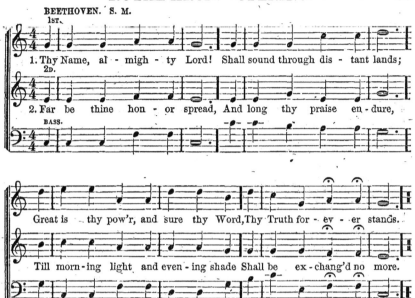

BEETHOVEN. S. M.

1. Thy Name, al - migh - ty Lord! Shall sound through dis - tant lands;

2. Far be thine hon - or spread, And long thy praise en - dure,

Great is thy pow'r, and sure thy Word, Thy Truth for - ev - er stands.

Till morn - ing light and even - ing shade Shall be ex - chang'd no more.

210 *Knight Templar. Opening.*

1 While my Redeemer's near,
    My Shepherd and my guide,
I bid farewell to every fear;
    My wants are all supplied.

2 To ever-fragrant meads,
    Where rich abundance grows,
His gracious hand indulgent leads,
    And guards my sweet repose.

3 Dear Shepherd! if I stray,
    My wandering feet restore;
And guard me with a watchful eye,
    And let me rove no more.

211 *Closing.*

1 Lord, keep us safe this night,
    Secure from all our fears;
May angels guard us while we sleep,
    Till morning light appears.

2 Lord, when our days are past,
    And we from time remove,
Oh may we in thy bosom rest,
    The bosom of thy love.

[5*]

212 *Closing.*

1 Lord, at this closing hour,
    Establish every heart
Upon thy word of truth and power,
    To keep us when we part.

2 Peace to our brethren give;
    Fill all our hearts with love;
In Faith and Friendship may we live,
    And seek our rest above.

3 Through changes bright or drear,
    We would thy will pursue,
And toil like faithful servants here,
    Till we thy glory view.

213 *Closing.*

1 Great God! impart thy power
    To every waiting heart;
Diffuse around a gracious shower,
    And bless us e'er we part.

2 Bless all who in this place,
    Have heard with earnest mind;
Give every brother here the grace,
    The way of life to find.

SHIRLAND. S. M.   Words by G. W. CHASE.

1. How charm-ing is this place; How plea - sant this re - treat;—

2. Thus may it ev - er be, While life and breath en - dure,

Where heart to heart, and face to face, True friends to - geth-er meet.

And we, from care and sor - row free, Safe reach the heav'nly shore.

215 *Dedication, or Consecration.*

1 Great source of light and love,
   To Thee our songs we raise!
O! in thy temple, Lord, above,
   Hear and accept our praise!

2 Shine on this festive day,
   Succeed its hoped design,
And may our Charity display
   A love resembling thine.

3 May this fraternal band,
   Now *Consecrated*—blest,
In Union all distinguished stand,
   In Purity be drest.

4 May all the sons of peace,
   Their every grace improve;
Till discord through the nations cease,
   And all the world be love.

216   *Opening.*

1 Kind Father! hear our prayer,—
   We bow before thy throne;
O may we find acceptance there,
   And peace before unknown.

2 Within these walls may Peace
   And Harmony be found;
May Faith and Charity increase,
   And Hope and Love abound.

217   *Closing.*

1 Now, brothers, we must part,
   Where we have met in peace,
Where harmony its joys impart,
   And strife and discord cease.

2 We on the Level meet,
   Upon the Square we part;
May Truth and Love, and Friendship sweet
   Pervade each brother's heart.

3 Here, Lord, before we part,
   Help us to bless thy name;
Let every tongue, and every heart,
   Praise and adore the same.

218   *Royal Arch. Closing.*

Thy *Name*, Almighty Lord,
   Shall sound through distant lands;
Great is thy power, and sure thy *Word*;
   Thy Truth forever stands.

219   *Closing.*

1 Lord, keep us safe this night,
   Secure from all our fears;
May angels guard us while we sleep,
   Till morning light appears.

2 Lord, when our days are past,
   And we from time remove,
Oh may we find in heaven a rest,
   In mansions of thy love.

AIR — "ALL'S WELL."_ Adapted by Bro. J. B. TAYLOR.

1. Pro-tect-ed by Ma-son-ic pow'r, In life's high noon, or fi-nal hour, As
2. De-pend-ent on Ma-son-ic aid, By Line and Com-pass lev-el made, The

one grand Lodge the world is found, And all mankind as brothers bound, And all man-
Mas-ter So-cial draws his plan, And calls to la-bor ev-'ry man: And calls to

kind as broth-ers bound, And all man-kind as brothers bound Their se-crets form a
la-bor ev-'ry man, And calls to la-bor ev-'ry man: While truth her sure foun-

mor-al store, The Ti-ler, si-lent, guards the door, The Ti-ler, si-lent,
da-tion lays, And by de-grees we mer-rit raise, And by de-grees we

guards the door, the guarded door, Who comes there? A brother seeks the light! The
mer-it raise, we mer-it raise, Who is there? A brother seeks the light! In

sign? the word? All's right, all's right, All, all's right, The sign? The word? All, all's right.
hand and heart, All's right, all's right, All, all's right, The sign? The word? All, all's right.

"INDIAN PHILOSOPHER." C. P. M.

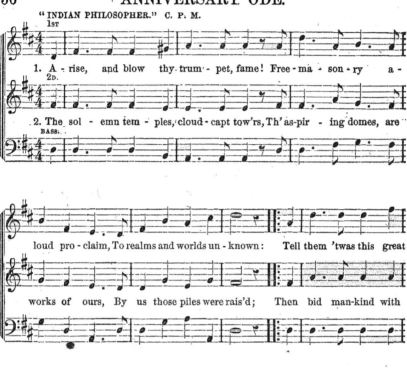

1. A - rise, and blow thy-trum - pet, fame! Free - ma - son - ry a -
2. The sol - emn tem - ples, cloud - capt tow'rs, Th' as-pir - ing domes, are

loud pro - claim, To realms and worlds un - known: Tell them 'twas this great
works of ours, By us those piles were rais'd; Then bid man-kind with

Da - vid's son, The wise, the matchless Sol - o - mon, Priz'd far a - bove his throne.
songs ad-vance, And thro' th' ethereal vast ex-panse, Let Ma - son - ry be prais'd.

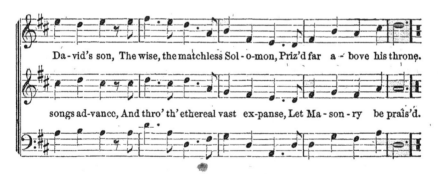

3	4
We help the poor in time of need,	Still louder, Fame! thy trumpet blow;
The naked clothe, the hungry feed,	Let all the distant regions know
'Tis our foundation stone:	Free-Masonry is this:
We build upon the noblest plan,	Almighty Wisdom gave it birth,
For friendship rivets man to man,	And Heaven has fixed it here on earth,
And makes us all as one.	A type of future bliss!

222. *Social Song.*

1 Convened we're met my jovial souls,
Then fill again the flowing bowls,
  Let concord be the toast;
With glass in hand, let each agree
To sing in praise of Masonry,
  What mortal more can boast.

2 Here dove-eyed peace, celestial maid,
Stands ready waiting us to aid,
  And guard our mystic door!
Here's charity, from heaven sent,
To bring her freeborn sons content,
  And comfort to the poor.

3 See, in the East effulgent shine,
Bright wisdom with his rays divine,
  Hark! hark the solemn sound;
While thus we live in mutual love,
We taste what angels do above,
  Here happiness is found.

4 The fruit of Eden's tree we taste,
Its balmy joys are our repast,
  Here freedom cheers the heart;
The indigent, opprest with grief,
Gains from his brother's hand relief,
  Each to his want impart.

5 The great and good, with us combine
To trace our mysteries divine,
  And find the pleasing light;
With pleasure we pursue the plan,
While friendship rivets man to man,
  How pleasing is the sight.

6 Till Heaven sends its summons forth,
From east to west, from south to north,
  Her chosen sons to call;
While time runs its continual round,
Shall fame with golden trumpet sound,
  Masons shall never fall.

223 *Masonic Ode.*

1 Hail, Mystic Light! whose holy flame
Can cheer the weak, the fierce can tame,
  And raise the trembling soul!
Hail, sacred source of human skill!
Hail, great director of the will!
  Star of the mental pole!

2 Hail, Masonry! thou first, thou last,
Of all the scope by mind embraced;
  Thou teacher, friend, and guide;
Around thine altar now we stand,
In union strong, a loving band;
  Thus will we e'er abide.

224 *Anniversary, or Installation.*

1 When darkness veiled the hopes of man,
Then light with radiant beams began
  To cheer his clouded way;
In graceful form, to soothe his woes,
The *Beauty* to his vision rose,
  In bright and gentle ray.

2 Immortal *Order* stood confessed,
From furthest *East* to distant *West*,
  In columns just and true;
The faithful *Plumb* and *Level* there,
Uniting with the mystic *Square*,
  The Temple brought to view.

3 Descending then from heaven, Most High,
Came *Charity* with tearful eye
  To dwell with feeble man;
Hope whispered peace in brighter skies,
On which a trusting *Faith* relies,
  And earth's best joys began.

4 Abroad was seen the boon of Heaven,
Fraternal *Love* was kindly given,
  And touched each kindred heart;
The *Sons of Light* with transport then,
In kindness to their fellow men,
  Unveiled the *Mystic Art*.

5 Let grateful peans loudly raise
O'er earth's domains, to azure skies,
  As time shall onward move;
A brother's joy and we shall be,
Undying bonds to mark the *Free*,
  To wake a brother's Love.

225 *Masonic Song.*

1 Divine Urania, virgin pure!
Enthroned in the Olympian bower,
  I here invoke thy lays!
Celestial muse! awake the lyre,
With heaven-born sweet seraphic fire,
  Free-Masonry to praise.

2 The stately structures that arise,
And brush the concave of the skies,
  Still ornament thy shrine;
Th' aspiring dome, those works of ours,
"The solemn temples—cloud capt towers,"
  Confess the Art divine.

3 With Prudence all our actions are,
By Bible, Compass, and by Square,
  In love and truth combined;
While Justice and Benevolence,
With Fortitude and Temperance,
  Adorn and grace the mind!

"DALSTON." S. P. M.

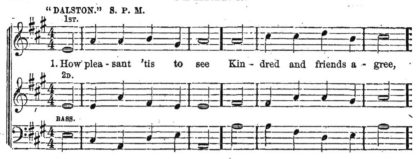

1. How plea-sant 'tis to see Kin-dred and friends a-gree,

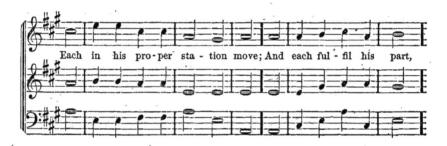

Each in his pro-per sta-tion move; And each ful-fil his part,

With sym-pa-thiz-ing heart, In all the cares of life and love!

2 Like fruitful showers of rain,
  That water all the plain,
    Descending from the neighboring hills;
  Such streams of pleasure roll
  Through every friendly soul,
    Where love, like heavenly dew, distils.

3 'Tis like the ointment, shed
  On Aaron's sacred head,
    Divinely rich, divinely sweet!
  The oil through all the room
  Diffused a choice perfume,
    Ran through his robes, and blest his feet.

227   *Opening.*

1 Oh God! thy love we praise;
  How bright its glories blaze!
    Oh! may we live and love as one;
  Our doubts and fears depart,
  In each and every heart
    The holy will of God be done.

2 Thanks, grateful thanks, we raise,
  To him who crowns our days
    With blessings numberless and free;
  In one united band
  Of brothers, hand in hand,
    Live we in love and Unity

LENOX H. M.

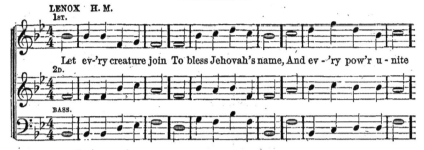

Let ev-'ry creature join To bless Jehovah's name, And ev-'ry pow'r u - nite

To swell th' exalted theme;   Let na-ture raise from ev - 'ry tongue A

Let na - ture raise from

Let nature raise from ev-'ry tongue A gen - 'ral song of

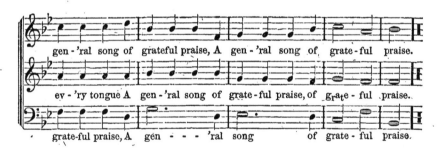

gen - 'ral song of grateful praise, A gen - 'ral song of, grate - ful praise.

ev - 'ry tongue A gen - 'ral song of grate-ful praise, of grate - ful praise.

grate-ful praise, A gen - - - 'ral song of grate - ful praise.

229   *Installation.*

1 Ye boundless realms of joy,
    Exalt your Maker's fame;
His praise your song employ
    Above the starry frame;
Your voices raise, Ye cherubim
And seraphim, To sing his praise.

2 United zeal be shown,
    His wondrous fame to raise,
Whose glorious name alone
    Deserves our endless praise.
Earth's utmost ends, His power obey:
His glorious sway The sky transcends.

230   *Anniversary.*

1 Give thanks to God most high,
    The universal Lord;
The sovereign King of kings:
    And be his grace adored.
Thy mercy, Lord, Shall still endure,
And ever sure Abides thy word.

2 God is our sun and shield,
    Our light, and our defence;
With gifts his hands are filled;
    We draw our blessings thence:
He shall bestow On Jacob's race
Peculiar grace, And glory too.

PLEYEL'S HYMN. 7s.

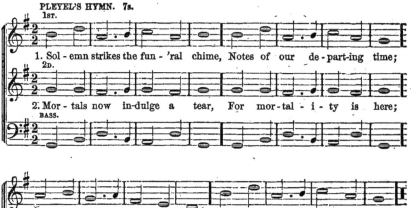

1. Sol - emn strikes the fun - 'ral chime, Notes of our de-part-ing time;

2. Mor-tals now in-dulge a tear, For mor-tal - i - ty is here;

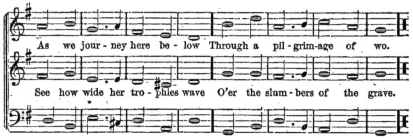

As we jour-ney here be - low Through a pil-grim-age of wo.

See how wide her tro-phies wave O'er the slum-bers of the grave.

3 Here another guest we bring!
  Seraphs, of celestial wing,
  To our funeral altar come,
  Waft our friend and brother home.

4 Lord of all below, above,
  Fill our souls with Truth and Love;
  As dissolves our earthly tie,
  Take us to thy Lodge on high!

232   *Closing, on any Degree.*

1 Lord of glory! King of power!
  In this lone and silent hour,
  Bid our feverish passions cease;
  Calm us with thy promised peace.

2 Sweetly may we all agree,
  In fraternal sympathy;
  Kindly for each other care;
  Every Brother do his share.

3 Sweetly may our spirits move,
  To the harmony of love;
  When our work of life is past,
  Oh! receive us all at last.

233   *Knights Templar. Closing.*

1 For a season called to part,
  Let us now ourselves commend,
  To the gracious eye and heart
  Of our ever-present friend.

2 Saviour! hear our humble prayer;
  Tender Shepherd of thy sheep!
  Let thy mercy and thy care
  All our souls in safety keep.

3 In thy strength may we be strong;
  Sweeten every cross and pain;
  Grant, that if we live, ere long,
  We may meet in peace again.

234   *Most Excellent Master.*

1 Suppliant, lo! we humbly bend,
  Father, for thy blessing now;
  Thou canst teach us, guide, defend;
  We are weak, but mighty thou.

2 Shed abroad, in every mind,
  Light celestial from above;
  Charity for all our kind,
  Trusting faith and holy love

235   *Opening.*

1 Met in Friendship's kindly name,
  We around our altar stand,
Owning each religion's claim,
  Bowing at her strict command.

2 Here our heartfelt prayers unite,
  For each Brother whom we love,
Blest with that pure Holy Light,
  Here reflected from above.

236   *Opening, or Closing.*

1 When the morning paints the skies,
  When the stars of evening rise,
We thy praises will record,
  Sovereign Ruler, Mighty Lord.

2 O how blest, how excellent,
  'Tis when heart and tongue consent,
Grateful heart and joyful tongue,
  Hymning thee in cheerful song.

237   *Closing.*

1 Lord, to thee our souls would raise
  Grateful, cheerful songs of praise;
And, when every blessing's flown,
  Love thee for THYSELF alone.

238   *Hymn for Installation.*

1 Unto thee, Great God, belong
  Mystic rites, and sacred song;
Lowly bending at thy shrine,
  Hail, thou Majesty divine!

2 Glorious Architect, above,
  Source of Light, and source of Love;
Here thy light and love prevail,
  Hail l Almighty Master, hail!

3 Still to us, O God! dispense
  Thy divine benevolence;
Teach the tender tear to flow,
  Melting at a brother's woe.

4 Heavenly Father, grant that we,
  Blest with boundless charity,
To th' admiring world may prove,
  Happy they who dwell in Love.

5 Join, oh Earth; and as you roll,
  East to West, from pole to pole,
Lift to Him your grateful lays,
  Join the universal praise.

[6]

239   *Opening.*

1 Lord! subdue our selfish will;
  Each to each our tempers suit,
By thy modulating skill,
  Heart to heart, as lute to lute.

2 Sweetly on our spirits move;
  Gently touch the trembling strings
Make the harmony of Love
  Music for the King of kings!

240   *Knights Templar.*

1 Angels! roll the rock away!
  Death! yield up thy mighty prey!
See! he rises from the tomb,
  Rises with immortal bloom.

2 'Tis the Saviour — seraphs, raise
  Your triumphant shouts of praise;
Let the earth's remotest bound,
  Hear the joy-inspiring sound.

3 Praise him, all ye heavenly choirs,
  Praise, and sweep your golden lyres
Praise him in the noblest songs,
  Praise him from ten thousand tongues.

241   *Master Mason.*

1 Hear my prayer. Jehovah, hear!
  Listen to my humble cries:
See the day of trouble near,
  Heavy on my soul it lies.

2 Hide not, then, thy gracious face,
  When the storm around me falls.
Hear me, O thou God of grace,
  In the time thy servant calls.

242   *Royal Arch. Closing.*

1 Lord, before thy throne we bend,
  Now to thee our eyes ascend:
Servants to our Master true,
  Lo! we yield thee homage due.

2 Low before thee, Lord, we bow,
  We are weak — but mighty thou:
Sore distressed, yet suppliant still,
  Here we wait thy holy will.

3 Leave us not beneath the power
  Of temptation's darkest hour;
Heavenly Father, yet be nigh,
  Lord of life and victory!

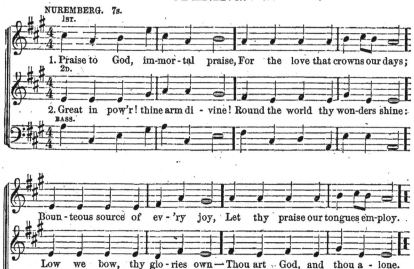

NUREMBERG. 7s.

1. Praise to God, im-mor-tal praise, For the love that crowns our days;

2. Great in pow'r! thine arm di-vine! Round the world thy won-ders shine:

Boun-teous source of ev-'ry joy, Let thy praise our tongues em-ploy.

Low we bow, thy glo-ries own—Thou art God, and thou a-lone.

244   *Royal Arch.*

1 Joy! the sacred Law is found,
  Now the temple stands complete,
Gladly let us gather round,
  Where the Pontiff holds his seat.

2 Joy! the secret vault is found;
  Full the sunbeam falls within,
Pointing darkly under ground
  To the treasure we would win.

3 This shall be the corner stone,
  Which the builders threw away,
But was found the only one
  Fitted for the arch's stay.

245   *Closing.*

1 Brothers, ere to-night we part,
  Join each voice and every heart;
Grateful songs to God we'll raise.
  Hymning forth our songs of praise.

2 Brothers, we may meet no more,
  Yet there is a happier shore;
Where, released from toil and pain,
  Brothers, we shall meet again.

246   *Opening.*

1 Lord, we come before thee now;
  At thy feet we humbly bow;
Fill our hearts with thy rich grace;
  Tune our lips to sing thy praise.

2 Comfort those who weep and mourn;
  Let the time of joy return;
Those who are cast down, lift up:
  Make them strong in Faith and Hope.

3 Grant that all may seek and find
  Thee, a God supremely kind:
Heal the sick, the captive free,
  Let us all rejoice in thee.

247   *Closing.*—G. W. CHASE.

1 Heavenly Parent! ere we part,
  Send thy blessing to each heart;
Make us loving, true, and kind;
  Make us one in heart and mind.

2 May we for each other care;
  Each his Brother's burden bear:
Fill our souls with Love divine;
  Keep us, Lord, forever thine.

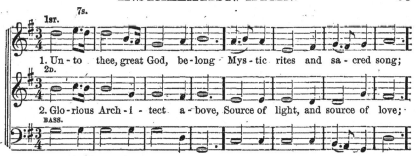

1. Un-to thee, great God, be-long Mys-tic rites and sa-cred song;
2. Glo-rious Arch-i-tect a-bove, Source of light, and source of love;

Low-ly bend-ing at thy shrine, Hail, thou ma-jes-ty di-vine.
Here thy light and love pre-vail, Hail, Al-migh-ty Mas-ter, hail.

3 Whilst in yonder regions bright,
The Sun by day, the Moon by night;
And the stars that gild the sky,
Blazon forth thy praise on high.

4 Join, oh Earth; and as you roll
From East to West, from pole to pole,
Lift to Him your grateful lays,
Join the universal praise.

5 Still to us, oh God, dispense
Thy divine benevolence;
Teach the tender tear to flow,
Melting at a Brother's woe.

249   *Opening, or Closing.*

1 Softly now the light of day
Fades upon our sight away;
Free from care, from labor free,
Lord, we would commune with thee.

2 Soon for us the light of day
Shall forever pass away;
Then, from care and sorrow free,
Take us, Lord, to dwell with thee.

250   *Hymn for Dedication.*

1 Lord, what offering shall we bring
At thine Altar, when we bow;
Hearts, the pure unsullied spring,
Whence the kind affections flow,

2 Willing hands to lead the blind,
Bind the wound, or feed the poor;
Love, embracing all mankind,
Charity, with liberal store.

3 Teach us, oh thou heavenly King,
Thus to show our grateful mind;
Thus th' accepted offering bring,—
Love to Thee and all mankind.

251   *Closing.*

1 When shall we all meet again?
Where shall we all meet again?
When the dreams of life are fled,
When its wasted lamps are dead:

2 When in cold oblivion's shade,
Beauty, wealth, and fame are laid,
Where immortal spirits reign,
There may we all meet again.

OPENING.

NASHVILLE. 7s.

S. B. BALL.

1. Soft-ly now the light of day Fades up-on our sight a-way;

2. Soon for us the light of day, Shall for-ev-er pass a-way;

Free from care, from la-bor free, Lord, we would commune with thee.

Then, from care and sor-row free, Take us, Lord, to dwell with thee.

253 *Opening.*

1 Softly fades the twilight ráy
Of another closing day;
Gently as life's setting sun,
When the Christian's course is run.

2 Night her solemn mantle spreads
O'er the earth, as daylight fades;
All things tell of calm repose,
Like the holy Sabbath's close.

3 Peace is on the world abroad;
'Tis the holy peace of God,—
Symbol of the peace within,
When the spirit rests from sin.

254 *Opening.*

1 Suppliant, lo! we humbly bend,
Father, for thy blessing now:
Thou canst teach us, guide, defend;
We are weak, but mighty thou.

2 Shed abroad, in every mind,
Light celestial from above;
Charity for all our kind,
Trusting faith and holy love.

255 *Opening, or Closing.*

1 Holy Spirit, from on high,
Bend o'er us a pitying eye;
Life and peace to us impart;
Dwell thyself in every heart.

2 May we constant grow in grace,
And with vigor run the race,
Trained in wisdom, led by love,
Till we reach our rest above.

256 *Opening.*

1 Holy Lord, lend now thine ear,
While our grateful song we raise;
May devotion, pure, sincere,
Mingle with our notes of praise.

2 Help us at this sacred hour;
Send the cares of earth away;
May we feel thy Spirit's power
While we chant our solemn lay.

3 Fill our hearts with holy fear,
While we feel thy presence nigh;
Let contrition's gentle tear
Moisten every brother's eye.

ERIE. 7s.

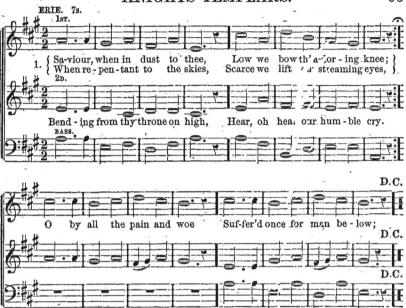

1. { Sa-viour, when in dust to thee, Low we bow th' a-dor-ing knee; }
{ When re-pen-tant to the skies, Scarce we lift our streaming eyes, }

Bend-ing from thy throne on high, Hear, oh hear our hum-ble cry.

O by all the pain and woe Suf-fer'd once for man be-low;

D.C.

258 *Opening, or Closing.*

1 Father! glory be to thee,
Source of all the good we see;
Glory for the blessed light,
Rising on the ancient night;
Glory for the hopes that come,
Streaming through the dreary tomb,
Glory for the counsel given,
Guiding us in peace to heaven.

2 Holy, holy, holy Lord!
Be thy glorious name adored;
Lord! thy mercies never fail;
Hail! celestial goodness, hail!
While on earth ordained to stay,
Guide our footsteps in thy way;
Then on high we'll joyful raise
Songs of everlasting praise.

259 *Closing.*

Thou from whom we never part,
Thou whose love is everywhere,
Thou who seest every heart,
Listen to our evening prayer.
Heavenly Father, through the night
Keep us safe from every ill;
Cheerful, at the morning light,
May we wake to do thy will.

[6*]

260 *Hymn, For Various Occasions*

1 Father of the human race,
Wise, beneficent, and kind,
Spread o'er nature's ample face,
Flows thy goodness unconfined:
Musing in the silent grove,
Or the busy walks of men,
Still we trace thy wondrous love,
Claiming large returns again.

2 Lord, what offerings shall we bring
At thine altars, when we bow?
Hearts, the pure unsullied-spring
Whence the kind affections flow;
Soft compassion's feeling soul,
By the melting eye expressed;
Sympathy, at whose control
Sorrow leaves the wounded breast: —

3 Willing hands to lead the blind,
Heal the wounded, feed the poor;
Love, embracing all our kind;
Charity, with liberal store:
Teach us, O thou heavenly King,
Thus to show our grateful mind,
Thus th' accepted offering bring,—
Love to thee and all mankind.

"ROSSEAU'S DREAM." 8s & 7s.

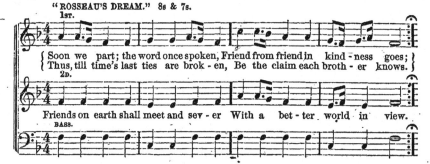

{ Soon we part; the word once spoken, Friend from friend in kind - ness goes; }
{ Thus, till time's last ties are brok - en, Be the claim each broth - er knows. }

Friends on earth shall meet and sev - er With a bet - ter world in view.

On the lev - el met, for - ev - er May we stand up - right and true;

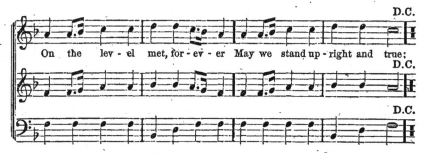

262 *Funeral Hymn.*

1 Cease, ye mourners; cease to languish
  O'er the graves of those ye love;
 Pain and death, and night and anguish,
  Enter not the world above.
 While in darkness ye are straying,
  Lonely in the deep'ning shade,
 Glory's brightest beams are playing
  Round th' Immortal spirit's head.

2 Cease, ye mourners; cease to languish
  O'er the graves of those ye love;
 Far removed from pain and anguish,
  They are chanting hymns above.
 Light and grace at once deriving
  From the hand of God on high,
 In His glorious presence shining,
  They shall never, never die.

263 *Closing.*

Lord, may angels watch above us,
 Keep us all from error free;
 May they guard, and guide, and love us,
 Till from earth we be set free.
May our footsteps never falter
 In the path the good have trod;
May we worship at the altar
 Of the great and living God.

264 *Encampment.*

1 Gently, Lord! Oh! gently lead us,
  Through this pilgrimage of tears;
 Through the changes thou'st decreed us,
  Till our last great change appears:
 When temptation's darts assail us,
  When in devious paths we stray,
 Let thy goodness never fail us,
  Lead us in thy perfect way.

2 In the hour of pain and anguish,
  In the hour when death draws near,
 Suffer not our hearts to languish,
  Suffer not our souls to fear;
 And, when mortal life is ended,
  Bid us on thy bosom rest,
 Till, by angel bands attended,
  We awake among the blest.

265 *Closing.*

Now, in gratitude abounding,
 May our hearts find sweet employ;
Every tuneful chord resounding
 With the notes of grateful joy:
May the tear of human sorrow
 Still through skies of mercy fall;
 Grant, oh Father, that the morrow
 May to fresh rejoicing call.

SICILY. 8s & 7s.

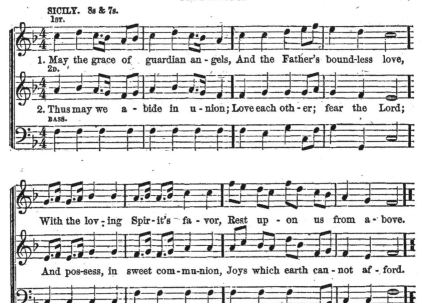

1. May the grace of guardian an - gels, And the Father's bound-less love,

2. Thus may we a - bide in u - nion; Love each oth - er; fear the Lord;

With the lov - ing Spir - it's fa - vor, Rest up - on us from a - bove.

And pos-sess, in sweet com - mu-nion, Joys which earth can - not af - ford.

267 *Fellow Craft. Work.*

1 Brothers, faithful and deserving,
    Now the second rank you fill,
Purchased by your faultless serving,
    Leading to a higher still.

2 Thus from rank to rank ascending,
    Mounts the Mason's path of love;
Bright its earthly course, and ending
    In the glorious Lodge above.

268 *Opening.*

1 Here all worldly cares forgetting,
    Every stormy passion stilled,
Angels bless us with their presence,
    And our souls with peace are filled.

2 Vainly break life's bitter surges
    'Gainst the walls that gird us in;
Only in the faintest murmurs,
    Comes to us their angry din.

3 Here, while heart to heart respondeth,
    Through the pulse's rhythmic beat,
Soul with soul, in fullest measure,
    Blendeth in communion sweet.

269 *Closing.*

1 Now we part! what sad emotion
    Fills each Brother's kindly heart,
As amid the world's commotion
    Each retires to take a part.

2 Let us, round this sacred altar,
    All our solemn vows renew;
Never waver, never falter,
    Each be steadfast, firm, and true.

270 *Charity.*

1 Meek and lowly, pure and holy,
    Chief among the blessed three,
Turning sadness into gladness,
    Heaven-born art thou, Charity!

2 Hoping ever, failing never,
    Though deceived, believing still;
Long abiding, all confiding
    To thy Heavenly Father's will.

3 Never weary of well doing,
    Never fearful of the end;
Claiming all mankind as Brothers,
    Thou dost all alike befriend.

PART IN PEACE.

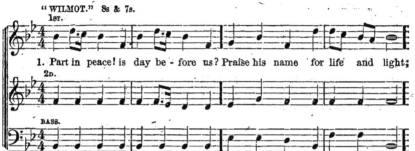

"WILMOT." 8s & 7s.

1. Part in peace! is day be - fore us? Praise his name for life and light;

Are the sha-dows length'ning o'er us? Bless his name who guards the night.

2 Part in peace! with deep thanksgiving,
Rendering, as we homeward tread,
Gracious service to the living,
Tranquil mem'ry to the dead.

3 Part in peace! such are the praises
God, our Maker, loveth best;
Such the worship that upraises
Human hearts to heavenly rest.

272 *Encampment. Opening, or Closing.*

1 Guide me, O thou great Jehovah!
Pilgrim through this barren land:
I am weak, but thou art mighty —
Hold me in thy powerful hand.

2 Open now the crystal fountain,
Whence the healing streams do flow:
Let the fiery, cloudy pillar,
Lead me all my journey through.

3 Feed me with the heavenly manna,
In this barren wilderness;
Be my sword, and shield, and banner;
Be my robe of righteousness.

4 When I tread the verge of Jordan,
Bid my anxious fears subside;
O'er its troubled waters bear me;
Land me safe on Canaan's side.

273 *Closing.*

1 Lo! the day of rest declineth,
Gather fast the shades of night;
Yet the sun, that ever shineth,
Fills our souls with heavenly light.

2 While, thine ear of love addressing,
Thus our parting hymn we sing,
Father, with thine evening blessing,
Rest we safe beneath thy wing.

274 *Closing.*

1 Part in peace! with deep thanksgiving,
Rendering, as we homeward tread,
Gracious service to the living,
Tranquil memory to the dead.

2 Part in peace! such are the praises
God, our Maker, loveth best;
Such the worship that upraises
Human hearts to heavenly rest.

BOUNDING BILLOWS. 8s & 7s.

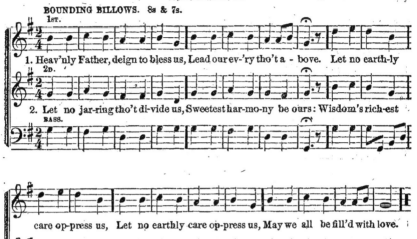

1. Heav'nly Father, deign to bless us, Lead our ev-'ry tho't a - bove. Let no earth-ly

2. Let no jar-ring tho't di-vide us, Sweetest har-mo-ny be ours: Wisdom's rich-est

care op-press us, Let no earthly care op-press us, May we all be fill'd with love.

feast provide us, Wisdom's richest feast provide us, As we pass these happy hours.

276 *Closing.*

1 Soon we part—let kind affection
  Be in all our acts displayed;
  Show by word, and deed, and action,
  Truth, and love, and friendly aid.

2 Soon will our Grand Master call us
  From this present bond of love;
  And, if *worthy*, will install us
  In the great Grand Lodge above.

3 Let us then, in bonds fraternal,
  Ever, ever onward move;
  Let our ties be the eternal
  Chain of Brotherhood and Love.

277 *The Kindred Few.*

1 If misfortune should o'ertake us,
  May we find a home with those
  Who may chide but not forsake us,
  Who will soothe our wants and woes.

2 Cast our lots with those who love us,
  Whose hearts tested, still prove true:
  Oh, may angel forms above us
  Ever guard the kindred few.

278 *Closing.*

1 Father, hear the prayer we offer;
  Not alone for peace we cry,
  But for grace, that we may ever
  Live our lives courageously.

2 Not within the fresh, green pastures,
  Will we ask that we may lie;
  But the steep and rugged pathway
  That we tread rejoicingly.

3 Be our strength in every weakness,
  In our doubt be thou our guide;
  Through each peril, through each danger,
  Draw us nearer to thy side.

279 *Closing.*

1 Lo! the day of rest declineth,
  Gather fast the shades of night;
  Yet the sun, that ever shineth,
  Fills our souls with heavenly light.

2 While, thine ear of love addressing,
  Thus our parting hymn we sing,
  Father, with thine evening blessing,
  Rest we safe beneath thy wing.

OPENING.

SCOTCH MELODY. 8s & 7s.

Words by G. W. CHASE.

1. Now, while evening shades are fall-ing Soft-ly o-ver land and sea,

2. Here in peace we meet to-geth-er, Face to face, and heart to heart;

While to *work* the gav-el's call-ing, Gent-ly call-ing you and me;—

Nought on earth can us dis-sev-er; In love we meet, In love we part:

Here we meet in chain un-bro-ken; Here we meet in friendship bright;

Lov-ing spir-its hov-er o'er us, Sweet-est har-mo-ny is ours;

Kind-ly word and friend-ly to-ken, Wait-ing here each "Son of Light."

Bright-ly shines the "Light" be-fore us, As we pass these hap-py hours.

281 *Closing Hymn.*

1 Now our festive joys are ending,
  And we all again must part;
Ere we go, our voices blending,
  Give the tribute of the heart:
Offer thanks, with grateful feeling,
  For our Father's love and grace,
For the truths, like plants of healing,
  For the wounds of all our race.

2 Let us each, the lessons heeding
  Of this holy festal time,
Strive by earnest prayer and reading,
  To possess the Truth sublime; —
Truth, that kindles like the shining
  Of the stars when eve sets in;
Truth far better for divining
  Than the rods and charts of men.

3 Now farewell! but ere retreating,
  Let us here, in union strong,
Vow we will not live defeating
  All that prompts to turn from wrong;
Then at last, on high ascending,
  Shall our anthems joyous rise;
With angelic voices blending
  Far above yon azure skies.

282 *Opening.*

1 When the light of day is winging,
  To this place we oft repair;
Here we all unite in singing,
  Here devoutly join in prayer:
While in harmony our voices
  Are ascending to our God,
Every grateful heart rejoices
  Thus to spread his praise abroad.

2 In the duties now before us,
  Let us faithfully engage;
May the light of Truth shine o'er us,
  Brightly from the sacred page:
Father! thus in pure devotion,
  Every thought inspired by love,
Gratitude in each emotion,
  Would we lift our souls above.

283 *Closing.*

Lo! the day at last declineth,
  Gather fast the shades of night;
Yet the sun that ever shineth
  Fills our souls with heavenly light.
While, thine ear of love addressing,
  Thus our parting hymn we sing,
Father, with thine evening blessing,
  Rest we safe beneath thy wing.

284 *Opening.*

1 Heavenly Father, gently bless us,
  Lead our every thought above;
Let no earthly care oppress us,
  May we all be filled with love.
Let no jarring thought divide us,
  Sweetest harmony be ours;
Wisdom's richest feast provide us,
  As we pass these happy hours.

2 Father! hear the prayer we offer;
  For repose we do not cry,
But for grace, that we may ever
  Live our lives courageously.
Be our strength in every weakness,
  In our doubt be thou our guide;
Through each peril, through each danger,
  Draw us nearer to thy side.

285 *Funeral Hymn.*

1 Cease, ye mourners; cease to languish
  O'er the graves of those you love;
Pain, and night, and death, and anguish,
  Enter not the world above.
While in darkness ye are straying,
  Lonely in the deepening shade,
Glory's brightest beams are playing
  Round th' immortal spirit's head.

2 Cease, ye mourners; cease to languish
  O'er the graves of those you love;
Far removed from pain and anguish,
  They are chanting hymns above.
Light and grace at once deriving,
  From the land of God on high,
In His glorious presence shining,
  They shall never, never die.

286 *Royal Arch. Closing.*

1 Humbly at thine altar kneeling,
  Hear us, Father, hear, we pray;
Thou whose eye doth watch us sleeping,
  Safely keep us through life's day.
Guide us, Heavenly Father, guide us;
  Cleanse our thoughts from every stain;
Let the grace of thy pure spirit
  Be our soul's delight and aim.

2 When our day of life is over,
  May we dwell with Thee above;
May we join with seraph's hymning
  Praise to thee — thou God of Love.
There, with angel harps and voices,
  May we swell the ceaseless song,
Ever happy, ever holy,
  Thou our God, and Heaven our home.

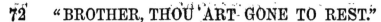

Slow. 7s, 6s, 8s & 6s.

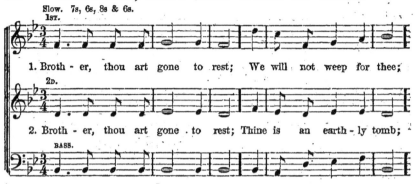

1. Broth - er, thou art gone to rest; We will not weep for thee;

2. Broth - er, thou art gone to rest; Thine is an earth - ly tomb;

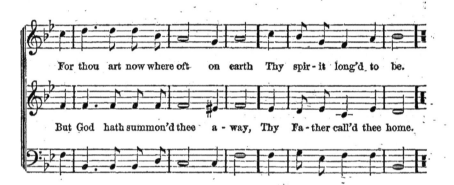

For thou art now where oft on earth Thy spir - it long'd to be.

But God hath summon'd thee a - way, Thy Fa - ther call'd thee home.

3
Brother, thou art gone to rest,—
Thy toils and cares are o'er;
And sorrow, pain, and suffering, now
Shall ne'er distress thee more.

4
Brother, thou art gone to rest;
Thy sins are all forgiven;
And saints in light have welcomed thee
To share the joys of heaven.

5
Brother, thou art gone to rest;
And this shall be our prayer,—
That when we reach our journey's end,
Thy glory we may share.

238   *Charity.*
"Then constant Faith and holy Hope shall
    die,
One lost in certainty, and one in joy;
Whilst thou, more happy power, fair Char-
    ity,
Triumphant sister, greatest of the three,
Thy office and thy nature still the same,
Lasting thy lamp, and unconsumed thy
    flame,
Shall still survive—
Shalt stand before the host of heaven con-
    fessed,
Forever blessing, and forever blessed."

289   *Closing.*—G. W. CHASE.
Brothers, as we part this night,
    May each devoutly pray,—
We all, among the "Sons of Light,"
    May meet in endless day.

8s & 6s.

1. Let there be Light! Th'Almigh-ty spoke! Re-ful-gent streams from cha-os

2. Pa-rent of Light! ac-cept our praise! Who shedd'st on us thy brightest

3. The wid-ow's tear, the or-phan's cry, All wants our rea-dy hands sup-

broke, T'illume the ris-ing earth! Well pleas'd the great Je-ho-vah

rays, The light that fills our mind! By choice se-lect-ed, lo! we

ply, As far as pow'r is giv'n; The na-ked clothe, the pris-'ner

stood, The Pow'r su-preme pronounc'd it good, And gave the plan-ets birth!

stand, By friend-ship join'd, a so-cial band, That love, that aid man-kind.

free, These are thy works, sweet Char-i-ty, Reveal'd to us from Heav'n.

In cho-ral numbers let us join To bless and praise this light di-vine!

In cho-ral numbers let us join To bless and praise this light di-vine!

In cho-ral num-bers, &c.

[7]

OPENING HYMN.

"GOD SAVE THE KING." 6s & 4s.

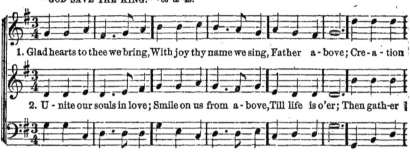

1. Glad hearts to thee we bring, With joy thy name we sing, Father a-bove; Cre-a-tion

2. U-nite our souls in love; Smile on us from a-bove, Till life is o'er; Then gath-er

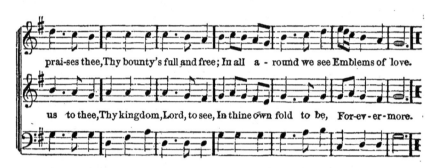

prai-ses thee, Thy bounty's full and free; In all a-round we see Emblems of love.

us to thee, Thy kingdom, Lord, to see, In thine own fold to be, For-ev-er-more.

292 *Mark Master.*

1. Mark Masters all appear;
Before the Chief O'erseer,
  In concert move;
Let him your work inspect,
For the Chief Architect;
If there be no defect,
  He will approve.

2. You who have passed the square,
For your reward prepare;
  Join heart and hand;
Each with his mark in view,
March with the just and true,
Wages to you are due,
  At your command.

3. Hiram, the widow's son,
Sent unto Solomon,
  Our great keystone;
On it appears the name,
Which raises high the fame
Of all to whom the same
  Is truly known.

4. Now to the westward move,
Where, full of strength and love,
  Hiram doth stand;
But if imposters are
Mixed with the worthy there,
Caution them to beware
  Of the right hand.

Ceremonies.

5. Now to the praise of those
Who triumphed o'er the foes
  Of Masons' art:
To the praiseworthy three,
Who founded this degree;
May all their virtues be
  Deep in our hearts.

293 *Closing.*

God of our Fathers, hear,
And to our cry be near,
  Jehovah, God!
While we before thee bow,
Forgive in mercy now,
Thy servants here, O Thou
  Eternal God.

294 *Knights Templar.*

1 God bless the worthy band,
Who grace this happy land
  With valiant Knights;
May the united Three
Of the blest Trinity,
Cement the Unity
  Of all great lights.

2 No Turk or Jew we'll fight,
But in Religion's right
  We'll breathe our last;
Entered, passed, raised, and arched,
And then like princes marched,
And though with rigor searched,
  Glorious we've passed.

3 Then Knights, clasp hand in hand;
In one united band
  We circle round;
May we e'er live in love;
May none unfaithful prove;
And finally, above
  May all be found.

295 *Anniversary Ode.*

1 E'er this vast world was made,
Or its foundation laid,
  Our Art begun;
Cherub and Cherubim,
Seraph and Seraphim,
Joined in one glorious hymn
  Before the throne.

2 God their Grand Master was;
Fixed their unerring laws;
  By his decree:
Faith, Hope, and Charity,
Friendship, and Unity,
Truth, Love, and Secrecy,
  All laws divine.

3 Oh may our constant theme,
To Heaven's Great King, Supreme!
  Be grateful Love:
May we whene'er we meet,
Chant Hallelujah's sweet,   *Three*
And three times three repeat   *times.*
  Jehovah's praise.

296 *Closing.*

When our last labor's o'er,
And scenes of life no more
  Charm our frail sight;
Then, in God's holy care,
May each protection share,
Bliss find unending there,
  In perfect light.

297 *Installation, or Dedication.*

1 Thou! who art God alone,
Accept before thy throne
  Our fervent prayer!
To fill with light and grace,
This house, thy dwelling-place,
And bless thy chosen race,
  O God! draw near.

2 As through the universe,
All nature's works diverse,
  Thy praise accord;
Let Faith upon us shine,
And Charity combine,
With Hope, to make us thine,
  Jehovah, Lord.

3 Spirit of Truth and Love,
Descending from above,
  Our hearts inflame,
Till Masonry's control
Shall build in one the whole,
A Temple of the soul
  To thy great name.

298 *Laying Foundation Stone.*

1 Let Masons' fame resound
Through all the nations round,
  From pole to pole:
See what felicity,
Harmless simplicity,
Like electricity,
  Runs through the whole.

2 When in the Lodge we're met,
And in due order set,
  Happy are we:
Faith, Hope, and Charity,
Love and Sincerity,
Friendship and Unity,
  Are ever free.

3 Long may our Craft be free,
And may they ever be
  Great, as of yore:
For many ages past
Masonry has stood fast,
And may its glory last
  Till time's no more.

299 *Doxology.*

To God — the Father, Son,
And Spirit — three in one,
  All praise be given!
Crown him in every song;
To him your hearts belong;
Let all his praise prolong —
  On earth — in heaven.

INVOCATION.

DORT. 6s & 4s.
1st.

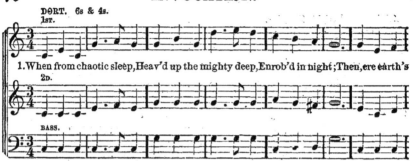

1. When from chaotic sleep, Heav'd up the mighty deep, Enrob'd in night; Then, ere earth's

2D.

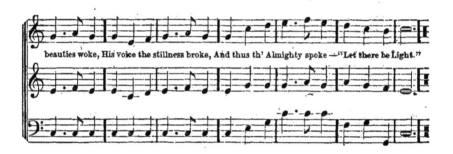

beauties woke, His voice the stillness broke, And thus th' Almighty spoke—"Let there be Light."

2 Swift from yon orb of day
Fled those dark shades away
  At his dread word;
Then sang the stars on high,
And through the arching sky
Swelled Heaven's loud minstrelsy,
  Praise ye the Lord.

3 Almighty power, supreme,
Send down thy brightest beam
  To every heart;
Illume us with thy grace,
Show us thy glorious face,
And Heaven's own righteousness
  To each impart.

301 *Closing.*

To Him who rules on high,—
Whose love is ever nigh,—
  All praise be given;
Let every heart adore,
Till on that blissful shore
We sing forevermore
  Secure in heaven.

302 *Encampment.*

1 Thou whose Almighty Word
Chaos and darkness heard,
  And took their flight—
Hear us, we humbly pray,
And where the gospel day
Sheds not its glorious ray,
  Let there be light.

2 Thou who didst come to bring,
On thy redeeming wing,
  Healing and sight,—
Health to the sick in mind,
Sight to the inly blind,—
Oh! now to all mankind
  Let there be light.

3 Spirit of truth and love,
Life-giving, holy Dove,
  Speed forth thy flight;
Move on the water's face,
Bearing the lamp of grace;
And, in earth's darkest place,
  Let there be light.

303 *Past Master.*

1 Come, and with generous will,
Past Master, bring your skill
Our work to prove;
Calm each invading storm,
Each erring thought reform,
With Truth each bosom warm,
Inspired by love.

2 Firm as our columns stand,
Be each approved command,
Where Brothers dwell:
Let notes of gladness roll
Over each trusting soul;
Far as from pole to pole
Let anthems swell.

304 *Invocation.*

1 Let there be light! said God;
And o'er the blooming sod
Broke forth the Morn!
Glad nature smiled in mirth,
While beauty filled the earth,
And flowers were born!

2 Let there be light within;
Then darkness, woe, and sin,
Your night is riven:
Then in pale sorrow's eye,
The starting tear shall dry;
O speed it, Heaven.

305 *Knights Templar.*

1 The laws of Christian light,
These are our weapons bright,
Our mighty shield;
Christ is our leader high,
And the broad plains which lie
Beneath the blessed sky
Our battle-field.

2 On, then, in God's great name;
Let each pure spirit's flame
Burn bright and clear:
Stand firmly in your lot,
Cry ye aloud, "Doubt not"!
Be every fear forgot;
Christ leads us here.

3 So shall earth's distant lands,
In happy, holy bands,
One brotherhood,
Together rise and sing,
And joyful offerings bring,
And heaven's eternal King
Pronounce it good.

[7*]

306 *Closing.*

When our last labor's o'er,
And scenes of life no more
Charm our frail sight;
Then, in God's holy care,
May each protection share,
Bliss find unending there,
In perfect light.

307 *Invocation. Encampment.*

1 Come, thou incarnate Word,
Come, thou our glorious Lord,
Our prayer attend;
Come, and thy servants bless,
Come, give thy cause success;
Spirit of holiness,
On us descend.

2 Come, holy Comforter,
Thy sacred witness bear,
In this glad hour:
Thou who Almighty art,
Now rule in every heart,
And ne'er from us depart,
Spirit of power.

3 To Thee, great One in Three,
The highest praises be,
Hence evermore;
Thy sovereign majesty
May we in glory see,
And to eternity
Love and adore.

308 *Anniversary, or Installation.*

1 Praise ye Jehovah's Name;
Praise through his courts proclaim;
Rise and adore;
High o'er the heavens above,
Sound his great acts of love:
While his rich grace we prove,
Vast as his power.

2 Now let our voices raise
Triumphant sounds of praise,
Wide as his fame;
There let the harps be found,
Organs with solemn sound,
Roll your deep notes around—
Filled with his name.

3 While his high praise ye sing,
Strike every sounding string;
Sweet the accord!
He vital breath bestows—
Let every breath that flows,
His noblest fame disclose:
Praise ye the Lord.

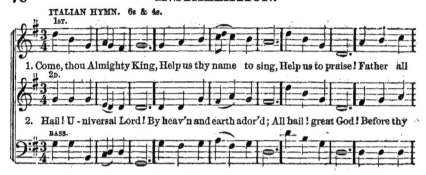

ITALIAN HYMN. 6s & 4s.
1st.

1. Come, thou Almighty King, Help us thy name to sing, Help us to praise! Father all

2d.

2. Hail! U-niversal Lord! By heav'n and earth ador'd; All hail! great God! Before thy

BASS.

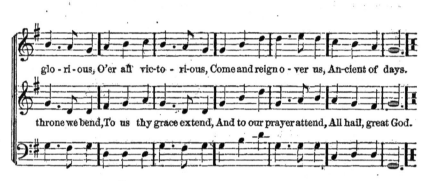

glo-ri-ous, O'er all vic-to-ri-ous, Come and reign o-ver us, An-cient of days.

throne we bend, To us thy grace extend, And to our prayer attend, All hail, great God.

310   *Invocation.*

1 Hail, universal Lord!
  By Heaven and earth adored,
    All hail, great God!
  From heaven, thy dwelling-place,
  Send down thy saving grace:
  Remember now our race,
    O Lord, our God.

2 God of our Fathers, hear,
  And to our cry be near,
    Jehovah, God!
  The heaven's eternal bow;
  Forgive in mercy now,
  Thy suppliants here, O thou
    Jehovah, God.

3 To thee our hearts now draw,
  On them write Thou thy law,
    Our Father, God!
  When in this lodge we're met,
  And at thine altar set,
  O, do not us forget,
    Our Father, God.

311   *Encampment. Installation.*

1 Glory to God on high!
  Let earth and skies reply;
    Praise ye his name!
  His love and grace adore,
  Who all our sorrows bore,
  Sing ye forevermore,
    Worthy the Lamb!

2 Join, all ye ransomed race,
  Our Saviour, God, to bless;
    Praise ye his name!
  To him our songs we bring,
  Hail him our gracious King,
  And, without ceasing, sing
    Worthy the Lamb!

3 Hail! Sovereign Prince of Peace!
  And may we never cease
    Praising his name;
  To him our songs we bring,
  Hail him our gracious King,
  And, without ceasing, sing
    Worthy the Lamb!

312 *Installation Ode.*

1 Hail! Masonry divine!
Glory of ages shine,
Long may'st thou reign;
Where'er thy lodges stand,
May they, have great command,
And always grace the land;
Thou Art divine!

2 Great fabrics still arise,
And grace the azure skies,
Great are thy schemes:
Thy noble orders are
Matchless beyond compare,
No art with thee can share;
Thou art divine!

3 Hiram, the Architect,
Did all the Craft direct
How they should build;
Sol'mon, great Israel's king,
Did mighty blessings bring,
And left us room to sing,
Hail! royal Art!

313 *Most Excellent Master. Opening.*

1 See from the Orient rise,
Bright beams to bless our eyes,
All hearts to cheer;
Let all with one consent,
Impelled by true intent,
Become Most Excellent,
In love sincere.

2 Bring songs of joyous sound;
Bring holy thoughts profound;
With hearts sincere:
Long be the Cap-stone found
Grateful to all around,
And notes of joy resound
In accents clear.

314 *Past Master.*

1 Come, and with generous will,
Past Master, bring your skill
Our work to prove;
Calm each invading storm,
Each erring thought reform,
With Truth each bosom warm,
Inspired by love.

2 Firm as our columns stand,
Be each approved command,
Where Brothers dwell:
Let notes of gladness roll
Over each trusting soul;
Far as from pole to pole
Let anthems swell.

315 *Closing.*

Spirit of Truth and Love,
Descending from above,
Our hearts inflame,
Till Masonry's control
Shall build in one the whole,
A Temple of the soul
To thy great Name.

316 *Installation, or Anniversary Ode.*
BY S. D. W. BROWN.

1 Hail! brother Masons, hail!
Let friendship long prevail,
And bind us fast;
May harmony and peace
Our happiness increase,
And friendship never cease,
While life doth last.

2 Sincerity and love,
Descendants from above,
Our minds employ;
Morality our pride,
And truth our constant guide,
With us are close allied,
And form our joy.

3 We on the level meet,
And every brother greet,
Skilled in our art;
And when our labor's past,
Each-brother's hand we'll grasp,
Then on the square at last,
Friendly we'll part.

4 May Wisdom be our care,
And Virtue form the square
By which we live;
That we at last may join
The Heavenly Lodge sublime,
Where we shall perfect shine
With God above.

317 *God Bless our Native Land.*

1 God bless our native land!
Firm may she ever stand,
Through storm and night;
When the wild tempests rave,
Ruler of wind and wave,
Do thou our country save,
By thy great might.

2 For her our prayer shall rise
To God above the skies;
On him we wait;
Thou who hast heard each sigh,
Watching each weeping eye,
Be thou forever nigh;—
God save the State!

MOST EXCELLENT MASTER.

11s.

By T. S. WEBB.

1st.

1. All hail to the morning that bids us re - joice; The tem-ple's com-plet-ed, ex -

2d.

2. Companions as-sem-ble on this joy-ful day, Th' oc-ca-sion is glo-rious, the

BASS.

alt high each voice, The cap-stone is fin - ish'd, our la - bor is o'er; The

key - stone to lay; Ful - fill'd is the promise, by th' Ancient of Days, To

sound of the gav-el shall hail us no more. To the power Almighty, who ev - er has

bring forth the capstone, with shouting and praise. There's no more occasion for lev - el or

guid - ed The tribes of old Is - rael, ex - alt - ing their fame; To him who hath

plumbline, For trow - el or gav - el, for compass or square; Our works are com-

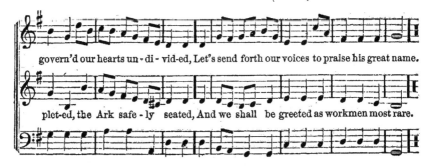

govern'd our hearts un - di - vid-ed, Let's send forth our voices to praise his great name.

plet-ed, the Ark safe - ly seated, And we shall be greeted as workmen most rare.

318   *Most Excellent Master.*

1 All hail to the morning that bids us rejoice;
  The temple's completed, exalt high each voice:
  The capstone is finished, our labor is o'er;
  The sound of the gavel shall hail us no more.

2 To the power Almighty, who ever has guided
  The tribes of old Israel, exalting their fame;
  To him who hath governed our hearts undivided,
  Let's send forth our voices to praise his great name.

3 Companions assemble on this joyful day,
  Th' occasion is glorious, the keystone to lay;
  Fulfilled is the promise, by the Ancient of Days,
  To bring forth the capstone, with shouting and praise.

Ceremonies.

4 There's no more occasion for level or plumbline,
  For trowel or gavel, for compass or square;
  Our works are completed, the ark safely seated,
  And we shall be greeted as workmen most rare.

5 Now those that are worthy, our toils who have shared,
  And proved themselves faithful, shall meet their reward.
  Their virtue and knowledge, industry and skill,
  Have our approbation, have gained our good will.

6 We accept and receive them, Most Excellent Masters,
  Invested with honors, and power to preside,
  Among worthy craftsmen, wherever assembled,
  The knowledge of Masons to spread far and wide.

Ceremonies.

7 ALMIGHTY JEHOVAH, descend now and fill
  This Lodge with thy glory, our hearts with good will:
  Preside at our meetings, assist us to find
  True pleasure in teaching good will to mankind.

8 Thy *wisdom* inspired the great institution,
  Thy *strength* shall support it till nature expire;
  And when the creation shall fall into ruin,
  Its *beauty* shall rise through the midst of the fire.

MOST EXCELLENT MASTER.

"THE TWINS OF LATONA." 11s or 12s.

1. All hail to the morn - ing that bids us re - joice;
2. To the pow'r Al - migh - ty,.... who ev - er has guided

The tem - ple's com - ple - ted, ex - alt high each voice:
The tribes of old Is - rael, ex - alt - ing their fame;

The cap - stone is fin - ish'd, our la - bor is o'er;
To him who hath gov - ern'd our hearts un - di - vided,

The sound of the gav - el shall hail us no more.
Let's send forth our voi - ces to praise his great name.

3 Companions assemble on this joyful day,
Th' occasion is glorious, the keystone to lay;
Fulfilled is the promise, by the Ancient of Days,
To bring forth the capstone, with shouting and praise.

Ceremonies.

4 There's no more occasion for level or plumbline,
For trowel or gavel, for compass or square;
Our works are completed, the ark safely seated,
And we shall be greeted as workmen most rare.

5 Now those that are worthy, our toils who have shared,
And proved themselves faithful, shall meet their reward.
Their virtue and knowledge, industry and skill,
Have our approbation, have gained our good will.

6 We accept and receive them, Most Excellent Masters,
Invested with honors, and power to preside,
Among worthy craftsmen, wherever assembled,
The knowledge of Masons to spread far and wide.

Ceremonies.

7 ALMIGHTY JEHOVAH, descend now and fill
This Lodge with thy glory, our hearts with good will:
Preside at our meetings, assist us to find
True pleasure in teaching good will to mankind.

8 Thy *wisdom* inspired the great institution,
Thy *strength* shall support it till nature expire;
And when the creation shall fall into ruin,
Its *beauty* shall rise through the midst of the fire.

320   *Masonic Song.*

1 When the sun from the East salutes mortal eyes,
And the sky-lark melodiously bids us arise;
With our hearts full of joy we the summons obey,
And haste to our work at the dawn of the day.

2 On the Trestle our Master draws angles and lines,
There with freedom and fervency forms his designs;
Not a picture on earth is so lovely to view,
All his lines are so perfect, his angles so true.

3 In the West see the Wardens submissively stand,
The Master to aid, and obey his command;
The intent of his signal we perfectly know,
And we ne'er take offence when he gives us a blow.

4 In the Lodge, sloth and dullness we always avoid;
Fellow-Crafts and Apprentices all are employed:
Perfect ashlers some furnish, some make the rough plain,
All are pleased with their work, and are pleased with their gain.

321   *Opening, or Work.*

Come, Craftsmen, assembled our pleasure to share,
Who walk by the plumb, and who work by the square;
While traveling in Love, on the Level of Time,
Sweet Hope shall light on to a far better clime

MOST EXCELLENT MASTER.

PORTUGUESE HYMN. 11s.

1. All hail to the morn - ing that bids us re - joice; The
2. To the pow'r Al - migh - ty, who ev - er has guided The

tem - ple's com - ple - ted, ex - alt high each voice: The cap - stone is
tribes of old Is - ra - el, ex - alt - ing their fame; To him who hath

fin - ish'd, our la - bor is o er; The sound of the Gavel, The
gov - ern'd our hearts un - di - vid - ed, Let's send forth our voi - ces, Let's

sound of the Gav - el, The sound of the Gav - el shall hail us no more.
send forth our voi - ces, Let's send forth our voi - ces, to praise His great name.

3 Companions assemble on this joyful day;
Th' occasion is glorious, the keystone to lay:
Fulfilled is the promise, by the *Ancient of Days*,
To bring forth the capstone, with shouting and praise.

Ceremonies.

4 There's no more occasion for level or plumbline,
For trowel or gavel, for compass or square;
Our works are completed, the ark safely seated,
And we shall be greeted as workmen most rare.

5 Now those that are worthy, our toils who have shared,
And proved themselves faithful, shall meet their reward.
Their virtue and knowledge, industry and skill,
Have our approbation, have gained our good will.

6 We accept and receive them, Most Excellent Masters,
Invested with honors, and power to preside,
Among worthy Craftsmen, wherever assembled,
The knowledge of Masons to spread far and wide.

7 Almighty Jehovah, descend now and fill
This Lodge with thy glory, our hearts with good will:
Preside at our meetings, assist us to find
True pleasure in teaching good will to mankind.

8 Thy *wisdom* inspired the great institution,
Thy *strength* shall support it till nature expire;
And when the creation shall fall into ruin,
Its *beauty* shall rise through the midst of the fire.

323
Installation Ode.

1 Behold! in the East our new Master appear,
Come, brothers, we'll greet him with hearts all sincere;
We'll serve him with freedom, with fervor and zeal,
And aid him his duties and trust to fulfil.

2 In the West, see the Warden, with Level in hand,
The Master to aid, and obey his command;
We'll aid him with freedom, with fervor and zeal,
And help him his duties and trust to fulfil.

3 In the South, see the Warden by Plumb stand upright,
Who watches the sun, and takes note of his flight.
We'll aid him with freedom, with fervor and zeal,
And help him his duties and trust to fulfil.

324
Faith, Hope, and Charity.
Faith.

1 There's a vision once seen never passeth from sight,
For it fixeth the eye, fills the soul with delight;
It clears all obstructions, admits of no shade,
Is a light to the mind — is a beam not to fade.

Hope.

2 There's a glow so seraphic, to gladden the earth,
We feel, while it lingers, its heavenly birth;
It blesses and cheers, soothes and comforts the world,
Embracing the globe, with its bright folds unfurled.

Charity.

3 There's a joy so absorbing, a rapture so calm,
It lives while there's impulse the heart's blood to warm
Nor quenched till the spirit shall part from the clay,
It illumes with its glory life's dreariest day.

[8]

86 COME, BROTHERS ACCEPTED. CLOSING.

"HOME, SWEET HOME." 11s.   Words by G. W. CHASE.

1. Come, Brothers Ac-cept-ed, come join in our song; In soft swell-ing meas-ure the glad notes prolong; Our la - bor is o - ver, the sum-mons has come, To lay by the trow - el, and hie to our home. Home, home, sweet, sweet home; We lay by the trow-el, and hie to our home.

2. In Friendship we meet, and in Friend-ship we part, U - ni - ted in pur-pose, u - ni - ted in heart; O thus be it ev - er, where'er we may roam, Till we meet, ne'er to sev - er, in Heav'n our home. Home, home, sweet, sweet home; Till we meet, ne'er to sever, In Hea - ven our home.

326 *Fellow Craft. Work.*

1 Come, Craftsmen, assembled our pleasure to share,
Who walk by the Plumb, and who work by the Square;
While traveling in love, on the Level of time,
Sweet Hope shall light on to a far better clime.

2 We'll seek in our labors the Spirit Divine,
Our temple to bless, and our hearts to refine;
And thus to our altar a tribute we'll bring,
While, joined in true Friendship, our anthem we sing.

3 See Order and Beauty rise gently to view,
Each brother a column, so perfect and true!
When Order shall cease, and when temples decay,
May each, fairer columns, immortal survey.

327 *Masonic Song.*

1 Oh! think not that life is the time for repose,
For the spirit to slumber, the eyelids to close;
Its hour is of actions, for heart and for hand,
No idle delay shall our progress withstand.

2 True joy will be found as the soul struggles on,
And life's wreath of glory unfading be won;
And wisdom shall shed o'er the spirit a ray,
Where beauty and freshness shall ne'er fade away.

328 *Closing.*

1 Farewell, till again we shall welcome the time
Which brings us once more to our fame-cherished shrine;
And though from each other we distant may roam,
Again may all meet in this, our dear loved home:
Home, home, sweet, sweet home,
May every dear brother find joy and peace at home.

2 And when our last parting on earth shall draw nigh,
And we shall be called to the Grand Lodge on high,
May each be prepared, when the summons shall come,
To meet our Grand Master in heaven our home:
Home, home, sweet, sweet home,
May every dear brother in Heaven find a home.

329 *The Mason's Home.*

1 Should the chances of life ever tempt me to roam,
In a Lodge of Freemasons I'll still find a home;
There the sweet smile of Friendship still welcomes each guest,
And Brotherly Love gives that welcome a zest.

2 When absent from Lodge, pleasure tempts me in vain;
I sigh for the moments of meeting again;
For Friendship and Harmony truly are there,
Where we meet on the level, and part on the square.

3 There the soul-binding Union surely is known,
Which unites both the peasant and king on the throne;
There the rich and the poor on the level do meet,
And, as brothers, each other most cordially greet.

4 On the quicksands of life should a brother be thrown,
It is then that the friendship of brothers is known;
For the heart points the hand his distress to remove,
For our motto is "Kindness and Brotherly Love."

5 When the Master of all, from his star-studded throne,
Shall issue his mandate to summon us home,
May each brother be found to be duly prepared,
In the Grand Lodge above us to meet his reward.

INSTALLATION ODE.

"THE BRIGHT ROSY MORNING." 11s.

By T. S. WEBB.

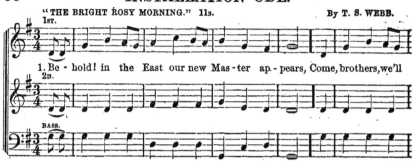

1. Be - hold! in the East our new Mas - ter ap. - pears, Come, brothers, we'll

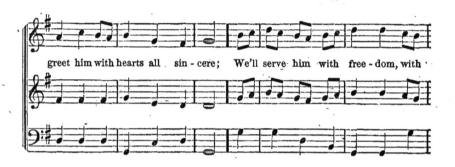

greet him with hearts all sin - cere; We'll serve him with free - dom, with

fer - vor and zeal, And aid him his du - ties and trust to ful - fil.

2 In the West see the Warden, with Level in hand,
The Master to aid, and obey his command.
We'll aid him with freedom, with fervor and zeal,
And help him his duties and trust to fulfil.

3 In the South, see the Warden, by Plumb stand upright,
Who watches the sun, and takes note of his flight,
We'll aid him with freedom, with fervor and zeal,
And help him his duties and trust to fulfil.

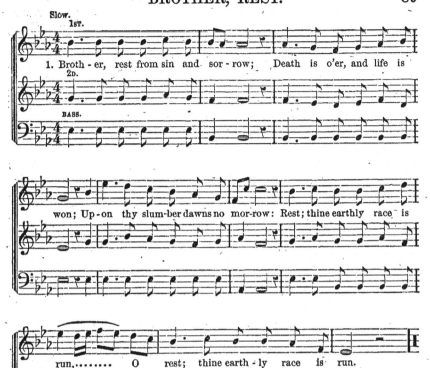

2 Brother, rest; the night is waning;
  Endless day is round thee poured;
Then enter thou the rest remaining
  For the people of the Lord.
  For, for the people of the Lord.

3 Fare thee well; though woe is blending
  With the tones of earthly love,
Then triumph high and joy unending
  Wait thee in the realms above.
  They wait thee in the realms above.

332 *We have met in Peace together.*

1 We have met in peace together,
  In this loved retreat again;
Our constant friends have led us hither,
  Here to join in tuneful strain;
  Here, here to join in tuneful strain.

[8*]

2 We have met, and time is flying,
  We shall part, and his swift wing,
Still sweeping o'er the dead and dying,
  Will the changeful seasons bring.
  Will, will the changeful seasons bring.

3 Let us, while our hearts are lightest,
  Look to Him who marks our years;
Rely on Him whose smile is brightest,
  And whose grace will calm our fears.
  Whose grace, whose grace will calm our
    fears.

4 He will aid us, should existence
  With its sorrows sting the breast,
While gleaming in the onward distance
  Faith will mark the land of rest,
  Our Faith will mark the land of rest.

"SCOTS WHA HAE." Words by G. W. CHASE.

1. Friends, the part - ing hour has come; Each must hie him to his home:
2. On the lev - el did we meet, Pass'd the hour in Friendship sweet,
3. Part we now up - on the square, Trust - ing in our Fa - ther's care;

Ere we go, be - fore the throne Let us hum - bly kneel.
Hap - py here a - gain to greet Each Ac - cept - ed one.
May each Craftsman's dai - ly prayer Reach the Mas - ter's throne.

Hum - bly ask the God of grace, To send down up - on the place,
Ere we part, join hand in hand; Firm - ly wo - ven, thus our band,
Till we meet in end - less day, So may each di - rect his way,

Bless - ings meet for ev - 'ry case; Ev - 'ry Broth - er's weal.
May each Broth - er faith - ful stand, Till life's la - bor's done.
He shall hear his Fa - ther say, Faith - ful ser - vant, come.

334 *Masonic Song.*

1 Friends and Brothers, swell the song,
Every voice the strain prolong,
Join in chorus loud and strong;
  On to victory:
Lift our banners, let them wave,
Onward still, the wretched save,
Smooth their pathway to the grave;
  Be their friend indeed.

2 Give the aching bosom rest,
Carry joy to every breast,
Make the poor and needy blest;
  Grant them kind relief:
Raise the glorious watchword high,
"Love! Relief! and Charity"!
Let the echo reach the sky,
  Swelling joyfully.

3 God of mercy! hear us plead,
Help us while we intercede;
Oh, how many bosoms bleed,—
  Heal them speedily:
Hasten then the happy day,
When, beneath thy gentle ray,
All the world shall own thy sway;
  Reign triumphantly.

335 *Bear Him Home.*

1 Bear him home, his bed is made
In the stillness of the shade;
Bear the Brother to his home;
  Bear, oh, bear him home.
Home, where all his toils are o'er,
Home, where journeying is no more
Bear him home no more to roam;
  Bear the Brother home.

2 Lay him down—his bed is here—
See, the dead are resting near;
Lay the wanderer gently down;
  Lay him gently down.
Lay him down; let nature spread
Starry curtains o'er his head;
Gently lay our Brother down;
  Gently lay him down.

3 Ah, not yet for us the bed
Where the faithful pilgrim's laid:
Through life's weariness and woe,
  Still our footsteps go.
Let us go, and on our way,
Faithful journey, faithful pray;
Boldly, Brother pilgrims, go!
  Boldly let us go!

336 *Opening.*

1 Brethren all, where'er you be,
Sons of Light, ye Masons Free,
Honor, Truth, and Virtue be
  Pride of Masonry!
Fervent zeal, with heart and hand,
Love-cemented, mystic band,
Firm, undaunted make us stand,
  Glorious Masonry.

2 Masons all, from pole to pole,
Love may guide, and truth control,
Sorrows come;—what can condole
  Griefs like Masonry!
Kindly smiling we have met,
Welcome each, and ne'er forget
Absent ones whom we regret,
  Friends in Masonry.

3 Craftsmen all, may love impart
Warmth into each honest heart;
Oft consult that faithful chart,
  Guide of Masonry.
When the spirit hence hath fled,
Angel guards their pinions spread,
Joyful crown each Mason's head,
  Heavenly Masonry.

337 *Patriotic Ode.*

1 Clime! beneath whose genial sun,
Kings were quelled, and freedom won:
Where the dust of Washington
  Sleeps in glory's bed,—
Heroes from thy sylvan shade
Changed the plow for battle blade,—
Holy men for thee have prayed,
  Patriot martyrs bled.

2 Crownless Judah mourns in gloom;
Greece lies slumbering in the tomb;
Rome hath shorn her eagle-plume,
  Lost her conquering name.
Youthful Nation of the West,
Rise! with truer greatness blest,
Sainted bands from realms of rest
  Watch thy brightening flame.

3 Empire of the brave and free!
Stretch thy sway from sea to sea;
Who shall bid thee bend the knee
  To a tyrant's throne?
Knowledge is thine armor bright;
Liberty thy beacon-light;
God himself thy shield of might,
  Bow to him alone.

8s & 6s.

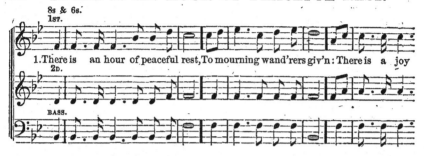

1. There is an hour of peaceful rest, To mourning wand'rers giv'n: There is a joy

for souls distress'd, A balm for ev'ry wounded breast, 'Tis found a-lone in heav'n.

2 There is a home for weary souls,
By sin and sorrow driven;
When tossed on life's tempestuous shoals,
Where storms arise, and ocean rolls,
And all is drear,—'tis heaven.

3 There Faith lifts up the tearless eye,
The heart no longer riven;
And views the tempest passing by,
The evening shadows quickly fly,
And all serene in heaven.

4. There fragrant flowers, immortal bloom,
And joys supreme are given;
There rays divine disperse the gloom;
Beyond the dark and narrow tomb
Appears the dawn of heaven.

339 *Opening.*

1 Blest is the hour when cares depart,
And earthly scenes are far!
When tears of woe forget to start,
And gently dawns upon the heart
Devotion's holy star.

2 Blest is the place, when Brothers bend,
And fervent prayers arise;
Where kindred hearts in union blend,
And all the soul's affections tend
Beyond the veiling skies.

340 *Hymn.*

1 This world is poor from shore to shore,
A baseless fabric given;
Its lofty domes and brilliant ore,
Its gems and crowns are vain and poor;—
There's nothing rich but heaven.

2 Empires decay, and nations die,
Our hopes to winds are given;
The vernal blooms in ruin lie,
Death reigns o'er all beneath the sky;—
There's nothing sure but heaven.

3 Creation's mighty fabric, all,
Shall be to atoms riven;
The skies consume, the planets fall,
Convulsions rock this earthly ball;—
There's nothing firm but heaven.

341 *Opening.*

1 Sing hallelujah to the Lord!
Sing with a cheerful voice;
Exalt the Lord with one accord,
Exalt the Lord with one accord,
And in his name rejoice.

2 May we to all eternity
Join in th' angelic lays,
And sing in perfect harmony,
And sing in perfect harmony,
Our great Creator's praise.

"NEAR THE LAKE."

Words by G. W. CHASE.

1. Now must close this friend - ly meet - ing, Each home to go;

3. As a - round our mys - tic al - tar, Bow we the knee;

Cheer - ful be our part - ing greet - ing, So soft and low.

Pray we Heav'n no heart may fal - ter; Each faith - ful be.

2. Bright the full orb'd moon sheds o'er us Her sil - ver light;

4. When at last the sum - mons wing - eth, "Ye ser - vants, come;"

Bright - er points the "Light" be - fore us, The way of right.

Hea - ven grant to each it bring - eth A wel - come home.

DO THEY MISS ME AT LODGE.

"DO THEY MISS ME AT HOME."   Words Adapted by G. W. CHASE.

1. Do they miss me at Lodge, do they miss me! 'Twould be an assurance most dear, To

2. When twilight ap-proaches the sea-son When oft we u - ni - ted in song, Does

3. Do they miss me at Lodge, do they miss me, When friendship's sweet pleasures are nigh, When

know that this moment some Brother Were saying, I wish he were here; To feel that the

some one repeat my name ever, And sigh that I tar - ry so long? And is there a

brightly the moon shines above them, And the hours pass pleasantly by; Are joys less in-

group round the al - tar, Are thinking of me as I roam, Oh! yes, 'twould be joy beyond

chord in the music, That's miss'd when my voice is away, A chord in each heart that a -

vitingly welcome, And pleasures less hale than before, Because one is miss'd from the

measure, To know that they wish I would come, To know that they wish I would come.

waketh Re - gret at my wea - risome stay, Re - gret at my wea - ri - some stay.

cir-cle, Be-cause I am with them no more, Because I am with them no more.

"AS THE EVENING SHADES DESCENDING." 95.

"JAMIE'S ON THE STORMY SEA."   Words by G. W. CHASE.

1. As the evening shade's des-cend-ing, Earth and sky to-geth-er blend-ing,

2. Now a-round the al-tar bend-ing, While all tho'ts are up-ward tend-ing,

3. Brightly shine the stars a-bove us; Warmly beat the hearts that love us;

Broth-ers true their way are wend-ing To their qui-et, lov'd re-treat:

Ev-'ry heart to heav'n is send-ing, Fer-vent prayers and grate-ful praise:

Firm we stand, a band of brothers, Link'd in Love and U-ni-ty:

Pleas-ant smile and friend-ly to-ken, Greet-ing warm, and kind word spo-ken,

Trust-ing Faith each bo-som fill-ing, Hope, like Her-mon's dew, dis-till-ing;

Wealth nor hon-ors here en-cum-ber; And when strikes the mys-tic num-ber,

Wait them there in chain un-brok-en, Wait them e'er when broth-ers meet.

Love, each e-vil pas-sion still-ing; Thus may ev-er pass our days.

Home we go to peace-ful slum-ber, Sing-ing "Peace and Har-mo-ny."

"HOW SWEET, WHEN SHADES OF EVEN."

"ANNIE LAWRIE."

Words by G. W. CHASE.

1. How sweet, when shades of e - ven Steal o'er the hill and plain; When the moon lights up the Hea - ven; To meet in peace a - gain, To meet in peace a - gain, A - mong th' Ac - cept - ed Free: Oh! the hap - pi - ness, dear Broth - er, To meet with such as thee.

2. We meet up - on the lev - el, What - e'er the name we bear; And when com - plete our la - bor, We part up - on the square, We part up - on the square, Like broth - ers true and free: Oh! the hap - pi - ness, dear Broth - er, To meet with such as thee.

3. Here Love, like sun of sum - mer, Im - parts both light and heat; There's not, where'er we wan - der, A - noth - er place so sweet, A - noth - er place so sweet, Nor hearts so true and free. Oh! the hap - pi - ness, dear Broth - er, To meet with such as thee.

MET AGAIN.

"HOME AGAIN."

Words by G. W. CHASE.

1. Met a-gain, met a-gain, in this lov'd re-treat, And

2. Trust-ing hearts, trust-ing hearts, here each oth-er greet, And

3. Friend-ship sweet, friend-ship sweet, lin-gers round the place, And

oh! it fills our souls with joy, Our broth-ers here to greet.

oh! be-side our hap-py home, There's not a place so sweet.

on each heart 'tis grav'd in lines That time can-not ef-face.

Here friend-ship beams from ev-'ry eye, And smiles on ev-'ry face:

The pride of wealth, the pride of birth, We keep with-out our door.

We meet in Peace, we work in Love, And part up-on the square:

There's naught on earth can break the tie That binds us to this place.

Re-ceive the humblest son of earth, If true,—we ask no more.

And un-to Him who rules a-bove, Lift up our voice in prayer.

CLOSING SONG.

AIR.—"THE SKY IS BRIGHT." Words by G. W. CHASE.

1. Our social labors now we close, And homeward quiet wend our way, wend our way; While

2. In works of char-i - ty and love, May each one act a brother's part, brother's part, Till

ev'ry bosom warmly glows, As sing we now our parting lay, parting lay. Good night,

all shall meet in Lodge above, And never more be call'd to part, call'd to part. Fare-well,

good night; We part in peace and on the square, and on the square, And this shall be our

farewell; Until we meet on that bright shore, on that bright shore, In mansions blest, our

parting prayer, our parting prayer: May Heaven bless each Brother dear, each Brother dear.

our la-bor o'er, our la - bor o'er, In mansions blest, our la-bor o'er, our la-bor o'er.

"MY MOTHER DEAR." Words by G. W. CHASE

1. How sweet, when shades of evening Steal o'er the land and sea, To meet up-on the

2. From all the world's commotion, Its troubles and its care; Here come to pass a

lev - el here, Among th' Accepted Free; Where kindly words and warm embrace A -

qui - et hour, We Brothers of the square. Here eye to eye, and heart to heart, We

wait each faithful heart: Oh! earth can boast no happier place, And no sub-li - mer

join in mys-tic rite; And when, up-on the square we part, 'Tis with a kind Good

Art. We're Broth-ers here; And this our prayer; Heav'n bless each Mason Brother.

Night. We're Broth-ers dear, And this our prayer; Heav'n bless each Mason Brother.

ROBIN ADAIR.

1. Broth - ers, we meet a - gain, Too soon to part;

2. Broth - ers, once more fare-well! 'Time bids us part;

May Friend-ship bless this hour, And warm each heart;

Fond mem -'ry long shall dwell A - round each heart;

Tones that we love to hear, Shall dwell up - on the ear,

May Heav'n its bless - ings send, And peace our paths at - tend;

As we in ac - cents clear Re - peat Good Night.

Un - til we meet a - gain, Fare - well, Good Night.

1. Good night, good night, and peace be with you, Peace, that gent-lest,
2. Good night, good night, but not for-ev-er, Hope can see the
3. Good night, good night, O soft-ly breathe it, 'Tis a prayer for

part-ing strain; Soft it falls, like dew on blossoms, Cher-ish-ing, with-
morn-ing rise: Many a pleas-ant scene be-fore us, As if an-gels
those we love: Peace to-night, and joy to-mor-row; For our God, who

in our bosoms, Kind de-sires to meet a-gain, Good night, good night.
hov-er'd o'er us, Bear-ing blessings from the skies, Good night, good night.
shields the sparrow, Hears us in his courts a-bove, Good night, good night.

COME, LET US HAVE.—CATCH.

1. Come, let us have a-noth-er song or two;
2. We'll sing this catch, and then I'll call on you;
3. For you can sing, I know, and so can you

[9*]

BONNIE DOON.   ROBERT BURNS.

1. A - dieu, a heart-warm, fond a - dieu, Ye brothers of the mys - tic tie;

2. Oft have I met your so - cial band, And spent the cheerful, fes-tive night;

Ye fa - vor'd and en - lighten'd few, Com - panions of my so - cial joy;

Oft hon - or'd with su-preme command, Pre - si - ded o'er the SONS OF LIGHT:

Tho' I to for - eign lands must hie, Pur - su - ing for-tune's slidd'ry ba';

And by that Hie - ro - glyph - ic bright, Which none but craftsman ev - er saw!

With melt - ing heart and brimful eye, I'll mind you still when far a - wa.

Strong mem - 'ry on my heart shall write Those hap-py scenes when far a - wa'.

3 May freedom, harmony and love,
Unite us in the grand design,
Beneath th' Omniscient *Eye* above,
The glorious *Architect* divine!
That you may keep th' unerring *line*,
Still rising by the *plummet's* law,
Till order bright completely shine,
Shall be my prayer when far awa'.

4 And you, farewell! whose merits claim,
Justly, that highest *badge* to wear,.
Heaven bless your honored, noble name,
To Masonry and Scotia dear!
A last request permit me here; —
When yearly ye assemble a',
One round, I ask it with a tear,
To him, the *Bard* that's far awa'.

BURNS' FAREWELL.

THE ORIGINAL AIR.

1. A - dieu! a heart-warm, fond a - dieu! Dear brothers of the mys-tic tie!

Ye fa - vor'd, ye en - light-en'd few, Com-pan-ions of my so - cial joy!

Tho' I to for - eign lands must hie, Pur - su - ing For-tune's slidd'ry ba',

With melt-ing heart and brim - ful eye, I'll mind you still, tho' far a - wa'.

NON NOBIS DOMINE.

A CELEBRATED CANON.   WM. BYRD. 1590.

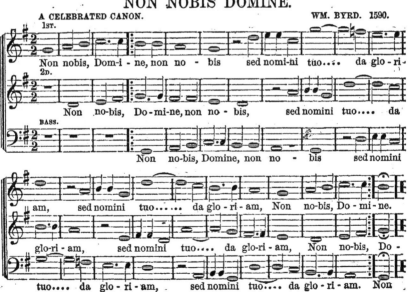

1ST.

Non nobis, Dom-i - ne, non no - bis sed nomi-ni tuo.... da glo - ri-

2D.

Non no-bis, Do - mi-ne, non no - bis, sed nomini tuo.... da

BASS.

Non no-bis, Domine, non no - bis sed nomini

am, sed nomini tuo...... da glo - ri-am, Non no-bis, Do - mi-ne.

glo-ri - am, sed nomini tuo.... da glo-ri-am, Non no-bis, Do -

tuo.... da glo - ri - am, sed nomini tuo.... da glo-ri-am. Non

CHARITY.

Moderato.

GLOVER.

1st.

1. Meek and low - ly, pure and ho - ly, Chief a - mong the bless-ed three,

2d.

2. Hoping ever, fail - ing never; Tho' de-ceiv'd, be - liev - ing still;

BASS.

rall:

FINE.

Turn - ing sad - ness in - to gladness, Heav'n-born art thou, Char - i - ty!

Long a - bid - ing, all con - fi - ding To thy heav'nly Fa-ther's will;

Pi - ty dwell - eth in thy bo - som, Kind-ness reign-eth o'er thy heart,

Nev - er wea - ry of well - do - ing, Nev - er fear - ful of the end,

D.C.

Gen - tle thoughts a - lone can sway thee, Judgment hath in thee no part.

D.C. only 1st. verse.

Claim-ing all man-kind as brothers, Thou dost all a - like be - friend.

D.C.

1. Brothers, sing with voice u - ni - ted, God speed the right: Join we now, with hearts de - light-ed, God speed the right. Lo! the winds in si - lence bear-ing, Lo! all na-ture's voice proclaiming, God speed the right, God speed the right!

<table>
<tr><td>

2

Be ye firm, and be enduring,
　God speed the right;
Always in the right pursuing
　God speed the right;
When all obstacles impede thee,
Trust in heaven for strength to aid thee,
　God speed the right.

</td><td>

3

When life's conflicts all are over,
　God speed the right;
May we ne'er prove faithless, never,
　God speed the right;
When all earthly ties are sundered,
When our days on earth are numbered,
　God speed the right.

</td></tr>
</table>

By T. S. WEBB.

SOLO.

1. I sing the Ma - son's glo - ry, Whose pry - ing mind doth burn,

Un - to com - plete per - fec - tion, Our mys - te - ries to learn;

Not those who vis - it Lodg - es To eat and drink their fill;

Not those who at our meet - ings Hear Lec - tures 'gainst their will.

DUETT.

But on - ly those whose plea-sure, At ev - 'ry Lodge, can be

T' im - prove them-selves, by lec-tures, In glo - rious Ma - son - ry.

CHORUS.

Hail! glo - rious Ma - son - ry! Hail! glo - rious Ma - son - ry!

Hail! glo - rious Ma - son - ry! Hail! glo - rious Ma - son - ry!

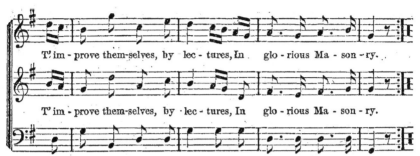

T' im - prove them-selves, by lec - tures, In glo - rious Ma - son - ry.

T' im - prove them-selves, by lec - tures, In glo - rious Ma - son - ry.

2
The faithful, worthy brother,
  Whose heart can feel for grief,
Whose bosom with compassion
  Steps forth to its relief;
Whose soul is ever ready,
  Around him to diffuse
The principles of Masons,
  And guard them from abuse;
These are thy sons whose pleasure,
  At every Lodge, will be
T' improve themselves, by lectures,
  In glorious Masonry.
CHORUS—Hail! glorious Masonry! &c.
3
King Solomon, our patron,
  Transmitted this command—
"The faithful and praiseworthy
  True light must understand;
And my descendants, also,
  Who're seated in the East,

Have not fulfilled their duty,
  Till light has reached the West."
Therefore our highest pleasure,
  At every Lodge, should be
To improve ourselves, by lectures,
  In glorious Masonry!
CHORUS—Hail! glorious Masonry! &c.
4
My duty and my station,
  As Master in the chair,
Obliges me to summon
  Each brother to prepare;
That all may be enabled,
  By slow, though sure degrees,
To answer in rotation,
  With honor and with ease.
Such are thy sons, whose pleasure,
  At every Lodge, will be
T' improve themselves by lectures
  In glorious Masonry!
CHORUS—Hail! glorious Masonry! &c.

MASONIC CANON.

Praise the.... Grand Mas - - - ter;

Praise the.... Grand Mas - - - - ter

Praise the.... Grand Mas - ter of the

U - ni - ver - - - sal Lodge.

2 The wisest of men was a Mason, we know,
From him our chief honors and dignities flow;
He founded the temple, the pillars he raised,
And Solomon still in our songs shall be praised.
CHORUS — Then join, brother Masons, &c.

3 With square and with compass, with level and line,
We constantly work to complete our design;
By prudence we steer, and the passions subdue,
What we learn in our youth, in our age we renew.
CHORUS — Then join, brother Masons, &c.

4 On freedom and friendship our order began,
To deal squarely with all is the chief of our plan;
The sneer then of fools we esteem as a feather,
Since virtue's the cement that joins us together.
CHORUS — Then join, brother Masons, &c.

5 Till the ocean be dry, and hard rocks melt away,
Till the globe shall dissolve, and no sun cheer the day;
So long shall the Masons their Order maintain,
And the arrows of slander be shot forth in vain.
CHORUS — Then join, brother Masons, &c.

1. Joy - ous, joy - ous now each heart's e - mo - tion,
2. Fa - ther, moth - er, of your love ye mind us,
3. Spir - it, bound - less! an - gels bow be - fore thee;

Ar - dent, ar - dent be the soul's de - vo - tion;
Broth - ers, broth - ers, to your hearts ye bind us;
Fa - ther, gra - cious! hum - bly we a - dore thee;

Swell the songs of grate - ful praise; Wel - come to this day of days:
Here we pledge our best re - turn, Love with - in our hearts shall burn,
Raise we now our grate - ful song, Thou our plea - sures dost pro - long,

Friend - ship, Friend - ship here is full as o - cean.
Ev - er, ev - er there 'till death shall find us.
Fa - ther! guide us, guide us, we im - plore thee.

[10]

Andante.

1. In his - t'ry we're told, how the Lodges of old A - rose in the

East, and shone forth like the sun; But all must a - gree, that di -

vine Ma - son - ry Commenc'd when the glo - rious cre - a - tion be - gun:

With glo - ry di - vine, oh, long may'st thou shine, Thou choicest of

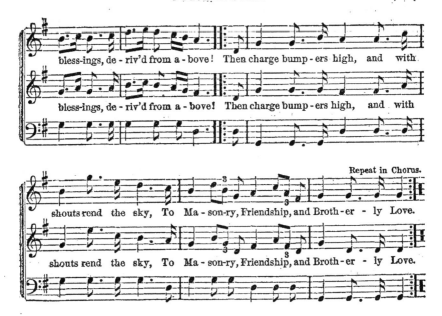

bless-ings, de - riv'd from a - bove! Then charge bump-ers high, and with

bless-ings, de - riv'd from a - bove! Then charge bump-ers high, and with

Repeat in Chorus.

shouts rend the sky, To Ma - son-ry, Friendship, and Broth-er - ly Love.

shouts rend the sky, To Ma - son-ry, Friendship, and Broth-er - ly Love.

2 Judea's great king, whose high praises we sing,
　With wisdom contrived while the Temple he planned;
　The mysterious art then took place in each heart,
　And Hiram and Solomon went hand in hand:
　While each royal name was recorded in fame,
　Their works earth and heaven did jointly approve;
　Then charge bumpers high, and with shouts rend the sky,
　To Masonry, Friendship, and Brotherly Love.
CHORUS — Then charge bumpers high, &c.

3 Then Masons were true, and the craft daily grew;
　They lived within compass, and worked by the square;
　In Friendship they dwelt, no ambition they felt;
　Their deeds were upright, and their consciences clear;
　On this noble plan Free-masons began;
　To help one another they mutually strove.
　Then charge bumpers high, and with shouts rend the sky,
　To Masonry, Friendship, and Brotherly Love.
CHORUS — Then charge bumpers high, &c.

4 These maxims pursue, and your passions subdue,
　And imitate those worthy Masons of yore;
　Fix a Lodge in each breast, be fair Virtue your guest,
　Let Wisdom preside, and let Truth tile the door;
　So shall we arise to an immortal prize,
　In that blissful Lodge which no time can remove;
　Then charge bumpers high, and with shouts rend the sky,
　To Masonry, Friendship, and Brotherly Love.
CHORUS — Then charge bumpers high, &c

AIR.—"GLORIOUS APOLLO."

Words by G. W. CHASE.

1. Full and har-mo-nious, Let the joy-ous cho-rus Burst from our
lips in one glad song of praise; Hail to the Art whose
glo-ry beameth o'er us; Loud to the heav'ns a-bove our voi-ces raise.
A - ges have pass'd since first our Art de-scend - ed, A - ges on

a - ges may it yet re-main; Join ev-'ry heart, in one full cho-rus

a - ges may it yet re-main; Join ev-'ry heart, in one full cho-rus

blend-ed; Long may our no-ble Art high state main-tain. Our no-ble

blend-ed; Long may our no-ble Art high state main-tain. Our no-ble

Art, Our no-ble Art, Our no-ble Art high state main-tain.

Art, Our no-ble Art, Our no-ble Art high state main-tain.

2

Loud let us sing, with heart and voice united,
Praise to the Architect of heaven and earth;
Him by whose word the stars above were lighted,
By whose Almighty breath our souls had birth.
Trusting his goodness, in his Word confiding,
Here to our altar grateful thanks we bring:
Firm in our purpose, in true Faith abiding,
Joining in chorus loud, our Art we sing,
Our Art we sing, our Art we sing,
In chorus loud, our Art we sing.

[10*]

HAIL! SUBLIME AND ROYAL ART.

"HAIL COLUMBIA."

Words by G. W. CHASE.

1. Hail! hail, Roy-al Art! Lov'd, re-ver'd by ev-'ry heart; Let thy praises tune our voice;

2. Raise, raise your voices high, Brothers of the mystic tie; Let the joy-ous cho-rus sound;

Let thy sons in thee re - joice; Let thy vir - tues in us shine; And prove thy or - i -

Let it e - cho all a - round, Let it peal o'er land and sea, Where'er may dwell th'Ac-

gin divine. Like the glo-rious orb of day, Brightly shin-ing on his way, Let thy light on

cepted free. Hearts u - ni - ted, hand in hand, May we ever firm-ly stand; Till we reach the

us descend To our la - test journey's end. Hail! sublime and Roy-al Art; Lov'd, rever'd by

Lodge a-bove, Faithful may each Brother prove. Hail! sublime and Royal Art; Lov'd, rever'd, by

ev - 'ry heart; Join we now in   praise to thee,Thou Art   of Arts, Free-ma-son - ry.

ev - 'ry heart; Join we now in   praise to thee,Thou Art   of Arts, Free-ma-son - ry.

363 *Hail! Hail the Mystic Tie.*

(BY BRO. S. WOODWORTH.)

1

Hail! hail the mystic tie,
Glorious orb of Masonry;
Like the orient beams of morn,
The bright empurpled East adorn,
To add effulgence to the day,
And drive the mists of night away.
Glorious source of light divine,
Friendship, peace, and virtue's shrine,
Songs of gratitude we raise;
Dedicate to thee our praise.
CHORUS.
Brothers, join the festive throng,
Social mirth inspires our song,
While in Harmony we meet,
And Masons all as Brothers greet.

2

See! see the darkness fly
Before the sun of Masonry;
Formed by heaven's almighty hand,
Its base as firm as earth shall stand,
Diffusing Light from East to West,
And nations with its beams be blest.
Arching ages round shall roll,
Time the fate of man control,
Still resplendent light shall stand,
Its summit reared by Virtue's hand.
Brothers join, &c.

3

Hail! hail, thou heavenly guest,
Sanctioned by the high behest,
Let Truth and Friendship be our guide,
Beneath whose compass we confide:
Our actions Squared by virtue's laws,
To magnify our first great cause.
Then, when life's meridian's past,
The tie of Friendship still shall last,
Its sacred Unity endure,
Till endless ages be no more.
Brothers join, &c.

364 *Patriotic Ode.*

1

Hail, Columbia, happy land!
Hail, ye heroes! heaven-born band;
Who fought and bled in freedom's cause,
Who fought and bled in freedom's cause,
And when the storm of war had gone,
Enjoyed the peace your valor won;
Let Independence be your boast·
Ever mindful what it cost,
Ever grateful for the prize,
Let its altar reach the skies.
CHORUS.
Firm, united let us be,
Rallying round our liberty,
As a band of Brothers joined,
Peace and safety we shall find.

2

Heroes, Patriots, rise once more,
Guard your rights, defend your shore;
Let no rude foe with impious hand,
Let no rude foe with impious hand,
Invade the shrine, where sacred lies
Of toil and blood the well-earned prize;
While offering peace, sincere and just,
Place in heaven your manly trust,
Truth and Justice shall prevail,
Every wicked scheme shall fail.
Firm, united, &c.

3

Sound again the trump of fame!
Let our Washington's great name
Ring thro' the world with loud applause;
Ring thro' the world with loud applause,
Let every clime to freedom dear,
All listen with a joyful ear;
With equal skill, with steady power,
He rules in the fearful hour;
Guides in horrid war, with ease,
And in times of honest peace.
Firm, united, &c.

"HAIL! TRIUMPHANT MASONRY."

AIR—"LIFE'S A BUMPER."

Adapted by Bro. J. B. TAYLOR.

"OUR FLAG IS THERE."   Words by G. W. CHASE.

1. High twelve has come! high twelve has come! The time to lay our a-prons by;

2. An hour for rest! an hour for rest! Our work-ing tools we now lay by;

High twelve has come! high twelve has come! The Sun has reach'd his sta-tion high.

An hour for rest! an hour for rest! While the sun is in the Southern sky.

The East has is-sued its de-cree, The West has e-choed Har-mo-ny,

Then shout a-loud, ye Craftsmen free, And let it e-cho o'er the sea;

The South to all th' Accepted Free, Has aloud proclaim'd, "High twelve has come."

'Tis time of rest for you and me, While th' sun is in the Southern sky.

368 *Here is Health for Lads and Lasses.*

1

Here is health for lads and lasses,
Sparkling in our crystal glasses;
  O, how cheerily it flows!
Health, that gushes from the fountain;
Health, that rushes down the mountain;
  Health, that blushes in the rose.

2

Drink, and hear the voice of duty;
Drink, and wear the robe of beauty!
  Beauty blossoms where water flows.
In the sweeping, weeping willow,
On the sleeping maiden's pillow,
  And the bosom of the rose.

[11]

369 *Here's a Health to all good Lasses.*

Here's a health to all good Lasses,
Pledge it merrily, fill your glasses,
  Let the bumper toast go round.
May they live a life of pleasure,
Without mixture, without measure,
  For with them true joys are found.
First Voice.
All good lasses.
Second Voice.
Here's a bumper.
First Voice.
Fill your glasses.
Second Voice.
Here's a bumper.
Here's a health to all good lasses, &c.

THE ENTERED 'PRENTICES' SONG.

From ANDERSON'S CONSTITUTIONS, 1723.

1. Come let us pre - pare, We Broth - ers that are As - sem-bled on mer-ry oc - ca - sion; Let's be hap - py, and sing, For life is a spring, To a Free and an Ac - cept - ed Ma-son.

2. The world is in pain, Our se - crets to gain, And still let them won-der and gaze on; They ne'er can di - vine The word or the sign Of a Free and an Ac - cept - ed Ma-son.

3 'Tis *this*, and 'tis *that*, They cannot tell *what*,
Why so many great men in the nation,
Should aprons put on, To make themselves one
With a Free and an Accepted Mason.

4 Great kings, dukes and lords, Have laid by their swords,
Our mystery to put a good grace on;
And thought themselves famed, To have themselves named
With a Free and an Accepted Mason.

5 We're true and sincere, And just to the fair,
They'll trust us on any occasion;
No mortal can more The ladies adore,
Than a Free and an Accepted Mason.

6 Then join hand in hand, By each brother firm stand,
Let's be merry, and put a bright face on;
What mortal can boast So noble a toast,
As a Free and an Accepted Mason? ⁀ *Chorus, three times.*

371

Of your Hearts to take Care.

1 Of your hearts to take care, now ladies prepare,
   Be silent; I'll tell you the reason:
  Sly Cupid, they say, as the most certain way
   To conquer the fair, is made Mason.

2 The music you hear will ravish your ear;
   Your eye will be pleased past expression:
  But think on the smart that follows the dart,
   When thrown by the hand of a Mason.

3 The nymph may pretend her heart to defend;
   But let her from me take a lesson:
  She's surely undone, though her heart were of stone,
   It will melt at one glance of a Mason.

4 By the apron and glove, Cupid reigns god of love;
   His empire to deny sure is treason:
  Then don't be ashamed, nor fear to be blamed,
   If you *should* fall in love with a Mason.

372

When Quite a Young Spark.

1 When quite a young spark, I was quite in the dark,
   And wanted to alter my station;
  I went to a friend, who proved in the end
   A Free and an Accepted Mason.

2 At the door then he knocked, which quickly unlocked,
   When he bid me to put a good face on,
  And not be afraid, for I should be made
   A Free and an Accepted Mason.

3 My wishes were crowned, and a Master I found,
   Who made me a most solemn oration;
  Then showed me the light, and gave me the right
   Sign, token, and word of a Mason.

4 How great my amaze, when I first saw the blaze!
   And how struck with the mystic occasion!
  Astonished I found, though free, I was bound
   To a Free and an Accepted Mason.

5 When clothed in white, I took great delight
   In the work of this noble vocation:
  And knowledge I gained, when the Lodge he explained,
   Of a Free and an Accepted Mason.

6 I was bound it appears for seven long years,
   Which to me is of trifling duration:
  With freedom I serve, and strain every nerve,
   To acquit myself like a Mason.

7 With hearty good will, let's show our best skill;
   To our Master pay due veneration;
  Who taught us the Art we ne'er will impart,
   Unless to an Accepted Mason.

HAIL TO THE DAY!

"HAIL TO THE CHIEF."

1. Hail, to the day! when as-sem-bled in Union, Springs at the al-tar of

Friend-ship and Truth, Pledge of our fair-est, our dear-est communion, The

flow-'ret, which blooms in pe-ren-ni-al youth. Hail to the day! when as-

sem-bled in Union, Springs at the al-tar of Friend-ship and Truth,

Pledge of our fair-est, our dear-est com-mu-nion, The flow'ret which blooms in pe-

ren-ni-al youth; E'er it has flourish'd fair, Sighed on by heaven's air,

Nur-tured by dew-drops, dis-till'd from a-bove, Bright o'er its na-tal bed,

Beams of gay light shall spread, Strength'ning the rays of Af-fec-tion and Love.

2 Hail to the Craft! whose light, broadly beaming,
   Streams from the loveliest *Star* of the sky;
O'er sorrow's vale ever cheerfully gleaming,
   Guiding to yonder bright temple on high;
Still may that holy ray, Type of immortal day,
   Light the lone path of the pilgrim along;
Till the Grand Master's 'hest, Bid all his labors rest,
   Attuning his harp to the mystical song.

3 Long may each Mason be firm in his duty,
   The grand and the useful in harmony join;
Long in his Temple may Wisdom and Beauty,
   Stars of the high arch of Masonry shine;
Here may we often meet, Each brother true to greet,
   Time strewing flowers o'er the swift-rolling year;
Here may fair Union rise, Here join the good and wise,
   Charity, Friendship, and Truth to revere.

4 Now to Creation's Great Builder ascending,
   Loud let the chorus of Gratitude swell;
Here, as before him we humbly are bending,
   O! may He deign in his Temple to dwell;
Here may the social fire Of love to heaven aspire,
   Long from this Altar rise incense of praise,
To the Eternal One, Our ceaseless shining sun,
   Master of all—Holy,—"Ancient of Days!"

"LIFE ON THE OCEAN WAVE."

Words by G. W. CHASE.

By permission of W. Hall & Son.

1. A place in the cir-cle for me; An hour with com-pass and square;

2. I come, when the full - orbed moon Looks down from her sta-tion a-bove;

3. Where'er my feet may roam, What - e'er my lot may be,

Where the heart is light and free, As the ea - gle in the air:

I come to our cho-sen home, With its Friendship and Brotherly Love:

In spir-it I oft will come, To my place in the Lodge with thee:

There is no place so dear; There are no hearts so true;

Here the pas-sions are subdued; With - in *due bounds* are seen;

In all the scenes be - low, In pleas-ure or in pain,

As those we meet with here, Though they be e'er so few.......

Here jealousy, envy, or feud, Ne'er come our hearts be - tween.....

My heart shall turn to you, And I'll long to meet again.....

[11*]

GLEE. "ALL HAIL! BLEST CRAFT."

"BEGONE, DULL CARE."   Adapted by Bro. J. B. TAYLOR.

1. All hail! blest Craft! Hail, Ma - son - ry di - vine, All hail, blest

2. All hail! blest Craft! while by thy light in - spired, We live by

Craft! how bright thy glories shine. Tho' fools a - gainst our or - der prate, And

square, by all wise men admired; Let those who know not our de - signs, A -

stig-matize our skill; I hold it one of the wisest things To be a Ma-son still.

buse us if they will; We hold it one of the wisest things To be a good Mason still.

3

All hail! blest Craft, long may thy glories shine
Through all the world, and prove the Art divine;
From East to West may all mankind,
Thy dictates mild fulfil,
And every brother hold it wise
To be a good Mason still.

Words by G. W. CHASE.

1. Hail! ye Craftsmen, join in chorus; Loudly let it e-cho o'er us; Glo-rious
2. Hap-py, hap-py is our meeting; Cordial is our mystic greeting; True and
3. Hap-py we and ev-'ry oth-er, Who can prove him-self a Brother; Nev-er

is the work be-fore us; 'Tis the work of Ma-son-ry. With our
warm each heart is beat-ing, As we cir-cle round our Light. Here our
can the world dis-cov-er How we talk by grip and sign: In the

voi-ces blending, We our cause de-fend-ing, On the air as-cending, Swell the
hearts are light-er, Here our hopes are brighter; Here we "grip" the tighter, Every
dark they're moping; They are blindly grop-ing, And in vain are hoping Our grand

| 1st time. | 2d time. | For last verse. |

anthems of the free!   Huz-za! huz-za!! huz-za!!!
wor-thy "Son of Light."   Huz-za! huz-za!! huz-za!!!
se-cret they may find.   Huz-za! huz-za!! huz-za!!!

1. Good night! good night! Now to all a kind good night!

Lo! the moon from heav'n is beaming, O'er the sil - ver wa - ters streaming,

'Tis the hour of calm de - light. Good night! good night! good night!

2 Good night! good night!
Now to all a kind good night!
Angel like, while earth is sleeping,
Stars above their watch are keeping,
As the star of Bethlehem bright.
Good night! good night! good night!

3 Good night! good night!
Now to all a kind good night!
Slumber sweetly till the morning,
Till the sun the world adorning
Rise in all his glorious might.
Good night! good night! good night!

Music from the GERMAN.

OPENING.

1. Oh come, come a-way, from la - bor now re - pos - ing; Let bu - sy care a-

2. From toil, and the cares on which the day is clos - ing, The hour of eve brings

while for-bear, Oh come, come a-way. Come, come our so - cial joys re - new, And

sweet re-prieve, Oh come, come a - way. Oh come where love will smile on thee, And

here, where trust and friendship grew, Let true hearts welcome you, Oh come, come away.

round the heart will gladness be, And time fly mer - ri - ly, Oh come, come a - way.

3 While sweet Philomel, the weary traveler cheering
   With evening song, her notes prolong,
        Oh come, come away.
   In answering songs of sympathy,
   We'll sing in tuneful harmony
   Of Faith, Hope, Charity,
        Oh come, come away.

4 The bright day is gone, the moon and stars appearing,
   With silver light illume the night,
        Oh come, come away.
   Come join your prayers with ours,
   Address kind heaven our peaceful home to bless
   With health and happiness,
        Oh come, come away.

8s & 6s.

1. Think gent-ly of the err-ing one! O do not thou for-get,
2. Speak gent-ly to the err-ing one! Thou yet may'st lead him back,
3. For-get not thou hast oft-en sinned, And sin-ful yet may be;

How-ev-er dark-ly stain'd by sin, He is thy Broth-er yet!
With kind-ly words, and tones of love, From mis-cry's thorny track.
Deal gent-ly with the err-ing then, As God has dealt with thee.

FAITH, HOPE, AND LOVE.

1. Though Faith may fee-bly guide thee, Yet raise thy droop-ing eyes,
2. Though Hope, thy side for-sak-ing, Per-chance may sleep or stray,
3. Though Love, when earth-ward flow-ing, May break the heart, or die,

Where shines, be-yond the skies, A sun to guide and light......... thee.
Yet he, who guards thy way, Is ev-er true and wak - - - - ing.
Yet an-gel's love, on high, Is ev er p ire and flow - - - - ing.

ROUND, FOR THREE VOICES.

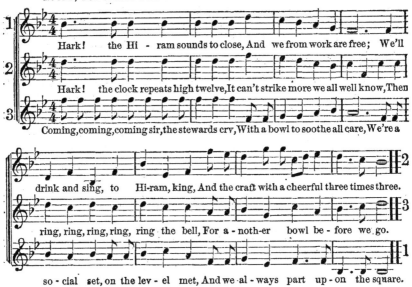

Hark! the Hi - ram sounds to close, And we from work are free; We'll

Hark! the clock repeats high twelve, It can't strike more we all well know, Then

Coming, coming, coming sir, the stewards cry, With a bowl to soothe all care, We're a

drink and sing, to Hi-ram, king, And the craft with a cheerful three times three.

ring, ring, ring, ring, ring the bell, For a - noth - er bowl be - fore we go.

so - cial set, on the lev - el met, And we al - ways part up - on the square.

"COME, SING THIS ROUND WITH ME."

A CATCH.

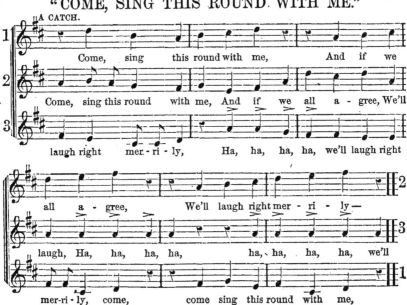

Come, sing this round with me, And if we

Come, sing this round with me, And if we all a - gree, We'll

laugh right mer - ri - ly, Ha, ha, ha, ha, we'll laugh right

all a - gree, We'll laugh right mer - ri - ly —

laugh, Ha, ha, ha, ha, ha, ha, ha, ha, we'll

mer - ri - ly, come, come sing this round with me,

OPENING, OR INSTALLATION CHANT.

By B. F. BAKER.

381

1 O sing unto the Lord a | new | song,
For he hath | done | marvelous | things.

2 With his own right hand, and with his | holy | arm;
Hath he gotten him- | self the | victo- | ry.

3 The Lord declared | his sal- | vation,
His righteousness hath he openly | showed, in the | sight of the | heathen.

4 He hath remembered his mercy and truth towards the | house of | Israel;
And all the ends of the world have seen the sal- | vation | of our | God.

5 Show yourselves joyful unto the Lord, | all ye | lands;
Sing, re- | joice, | and give | thanks.

6 Praise the Lord, up- | on the | harp;
Sing to the harp, with a | psalm | of thanks- | giving.

7 With trumpets | also, and | shawms;
O show yourselves joyful, be- | fore the | Lord, the | king.

8 Let the sea make a noise, and all that | therein | is,
The round world, and | they that | dwell there- | in.

9 Let the floods clap their hands, and let the hills be joyful together be- |
fore the | Lord:
For he | cometh to | judge the | earth.

10 With righteousness shall he | judge the | world;
And the | people | with | equity.

By S. B. BALL.

382

1   Hear! Father, hear our prayer!
Thou who art Pity where | sorrow pre- | vaileth,
Thou who art Safety, when mortal help faileth,
  Strength to the feeble, and | Hope to de- | spair;
Hear! Father, hear our prayer!

2   Hear! Father, hear our prayer!
Wandering unknown in the | land of the | stranger,
Be with all travelers in sickness or danger,
  Guard thou their path, guide their | feet from the | snare.
Hear! Father, hear our prayer!

3   Dry thou the mourner's tear;
Heal thou the wounds of time- | hallowed af- | fection;
Grant to the widow and orphan protection;
  Be in their trouble a | friend ever | near.
Dry thou the mourner's tear.

4   Hear! Father, hear our prayer!
Long hath thy goodness our | footsteps at- | tended;
Be with the pilgrim whose journey is ended;
  When at thy summons, for | death we pre- | pare,
Hear! Father, hear our prayer!

THE LORD'S PRAYER.

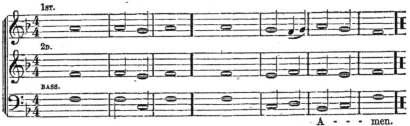

383

1 Our Father, who art in heaven, hallowed | be thy | name;
Thy kingdom come, thy will be done in | earth as it | is in | heaven.

2 Give us this day our | daily | bread,
And forgive us our trespasses, as we forgive | those that | trespass a- | gainst us.

3 And lead us not into temptation, but de- | liver us | from evil;
For thine is the kingdom, and the power, and | glory, for- | ever and | ever.

[12]

A PATRIOTIC SONG.

CHORUS.

O say does that star - span - gled ban - ner yet wave,

O say does that star - span - gled ban - ner yet wave,

O'er the land of the free, and the home of the brave.

O'er the land of the free, and the home of the brave.

2

On the shore dimly seen through the mists of the deep,
  Where the foe's haughty host in dread silence reposes;
What is that which the breeze, o'er the towering steep,
  As it fitfully blows, half conceals, half discloses;
Now it catches the gleam of the morning's first beam,
In full glory reflected, now shines in the stream —
  'Tis the star spangled banner, O long may it wave
  O'er the land of the free, and the home of the brave

3

And where is that band, who so vauntingly swore
  That the havoc of war and the battle's confusion,
A home and a country shall leave us no more;
  Their blood has washed out their foul footstep's pollution
No refuge could save the hireling and slave
From the terror of flight, or the gloom of the grave;
  And the star spangled banner in triumph doth wave
  O'er the land of the free, and the home of the brave.

4

O thus be it ever, when freemen shall stand
  Between their loved home and the war's desolation;
Blest with victory and peace, may the heaven-rescued land
  Praise the Power that hath made and preserved us a nation:
Then conquer we must, when our cause it is just,
And this be our motto —" In God is our trust,"—
  And the star spangled banner in triumph shall wave
  O'er the land of the free, and the home of the brave.

THE WISE MEN WERE BUT SEVEN.—CATCH.

"HOW GREAT IS THE PLEASURE."—CATCH.

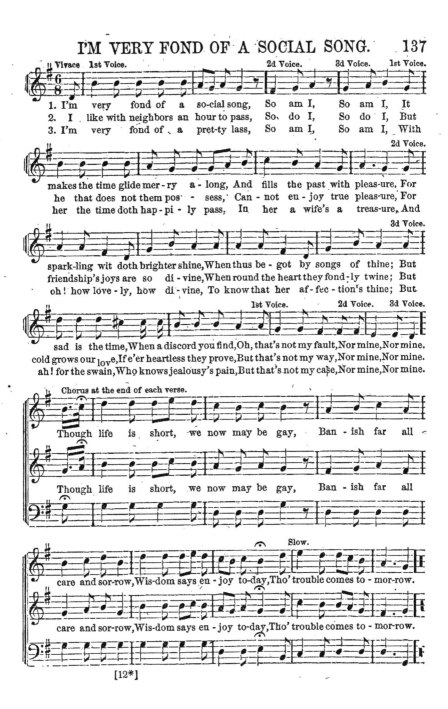

1. I'm very fond of a so-cial song, So am I, So am I, It
2. I like with neighbors an hour to pass, So, do I, So do I, But
3. I'm very fond of a pret-ty lass, So am I, So am I, With

makes the time glide mer-ry a-long, And fills the past with pleas-ure, For
he that does not them pos - sess, Can - not en-joy true pleas-ure, For
her the time doth hap-pi-ly pass, In her a wife's a treas-ure, And

spark-ling wit doth brighter shine, When thus be-got by songs of thine; But
friendship's joys are so di-vine, When round the heart they fond-ly twine; But
oh! how love-ly, how di-vine, To know that her af-fec-tion's thine; But

sad is the time, When a discord you find, Oh, that's not my fault, Nor mine, Nor mine.
cold grows our love, If e'er heartless they prove, But that's not my way, Nor mine, Nor mine.
ah! for the swain, Who knows jealousy's pain, But that's not my case, Nor mine, Nor mine.

Chorus at the end of each verse.

Though life is short, we now may be gay, Ban-ish far all

Though life is short, we now may be gay, Ban-ish far all

care and sor-row, Wis-dom says en-joy to-day, Tho' trouble comes to-mor-row.

care and sor-row, Wis-dom says en-joy to-day, Tho' trouble comes to-mor-row.

[12*]

HAPPY TO MEET.*

Music by S. M. DOWNS.

Words by G. W. CHASE.

1. Happy to meet, dear Brother mine, Up-on our checker'd floor; Happy to grasp that

2. Happy to leave the world awhile,—Its troubles and its care;—Happy to meet, and

hand of thine, And spend a so - cial hour: Happy to meet, tho' brief the stay That

here beguile An hour with plumb and square. Happy to meet, oh hap-pier we Than

we to-geth-er be; Hap-py to flee from care away, To meet with such as thee.

worldlings e'er can know, Happy to meet with Brothers free, Where comes not pomp or show.

3 Sorry to part, though down the West
   The evening sun descends;
Sorry to leave each welcome guest,
   Sorry to part with friends.
Sorry to hear the gavel's sound,
   That tells a "closing" nigh;
Sorry we circle the "Lights" around;
   Sorry we say "Good bye."

4 Sorry we halt around the door,
   Thy flight deplore, O Time;
Sooner we think than e'er before
   Did peal the signal chime.
"Happy to meet again," we part,
   Each wending home his way;
Hoping at last, with each true heart,
   To meet in endless day.

* "Happy to meet; sorry to part; happy to meet again."— *Old Masonic Toast.*

THE DEAREST SPOT IS HOME.

Words by J. B. TAYLOR.

1st.

1. The sa - cred spot to Ma - sons dear, Is in the Lodge!

2d.

2. When Broth - ers on the lev - el meet, With - in the Lodge!

BASS.

3. All praise to our Great Mas - ter rise With - in the Lodge!

The place where dwells not strife or fear, Is in the Lodge!

And friends and neigh - bors kind - ly greet, With - in the Lodge!

Re-sound his praise from earth to skies, With - in the Lodge!

God's pure laws the Craft re - ver - ing, Death they learn is

Sa - cred rites and forms u - nite us, Scrip - ture truths to

May each crea - ture of his pow - er, When the clouds of

D.C.

ever near-ing, Yet it doth no use - less tear bring Within the Lodge.

D.C.

search in-cite us, Virtue's course to lead invite us With - in the Lodge.*

D.C.

for - tune low - er, As - pi - ra-tions raise each hour With - in the Lodge.

* D.C. in words of 1st verse.

THE LEVEL AND THE SQUARE.

Written by Bro. ROB. MORRIS. Music by Bro. B. F. BAKER.

1. We meet up-on the Lev-el, and we part up-on the Square; What words of precious
2. We meet up-on the Lev-el, tho' from ev-'ry sta-tion come, The king from out his

meaning those words Ma-son-ic are! Come let us contemplate them, they are
palace, and the poor man from his home; For the one must leave his dia-dem out-

worthy of our tho't, With the highest and the low-est, and the rarest they are fraught.
side the Mason's door, And the other find his true respect up-on the checkered floor.

3 We part upon the square, for the world must have its due,
We mingle with the multitude, a cold, unfriendly crew;
But the influence of our gatherings in memory is green,
And we long upon the level to renew the happy scene.

4 There's a world where all are equal; we are hurrying to it fast,
We shall meet upon the level there, when the gates of death are past:
We shall stand before the Orient, and our Master will be there,
To try the blocks we offer by His own unerring square.

5 We shall meet upon the level there; but never thence depart;
There's a mansion—'tis all ready for each trusting, faithful heart;
There's a mansion and a welcome, and a multitude is there,—
Who have met upon the level, and been tried upon the square.

6 Let us meet upon the level, then, while laboring patient here,
Let us meet, and let us labor, though the labor be severe;
Already in the western sky the signs bid us prepare
To gather up our working tools, and part upon the square.

7 Hands round, ye faithful Masons, form the bright fraternal chain;
We part upon the square below to meet in heaven again.
Oh! what words of precious meaning those words Masonic are,
We meet upon the level and we part upon the square.

Music by S. M. DOWNS.   Words by BRO. O. S. SAUNDERS, M. D.

1. Let the mor - al of Ma - sonry twine round our heart; Behold how of earth all the glo - ries de-part; Our visions are fad-ing, our
hopes but a gleam, Our staff but a reed, and our lives but a dream.

2. Then, O, let us look—let our pros - pects al - lure— To
scenes that can fade not, to realms that en-dure; To glo - ries and blessings that
tri-umph sub-lime, On the blightening of change, and ru - ins of time.

PLEYEL'S HYMN.

Arranged as a March, by S. M. DOWNS.

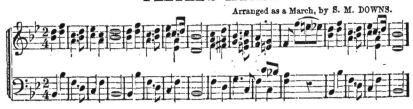

MASONIC FUNERAL MARCH.

Composed for this Work, by S. M. Downs.

TEMPLARS' GRAND MARCH.

Composed for this Work, by S. M. DOWNS.

393 *An Hour with You.*

(BY BRO. ROB. MORRIS.)

Music,—Auld Lang Syne.

1 An hour with you, an hour with you,
No care, or doubt, or strife,—
Is worth a weary year of woe,
In all that sweetens life;
One hour with you, and you, and you,
Bright links in mystic chain;
Oh may we oft these joys renew,
And often meet again.

2 Your eyes with love's own language free,
Your hand grips strong and true,
Your tongues, your hearts, do welcome me,
To spend an hour with you.
One hour with you, &c.

3 I come, when Eastern skies are bright,
To work my Mason's due;
To labor, is my chief delight,
And spend an hour with you.
One hour with you, &c.

4 I go when evening gilds the West,
I breathe the fond adieu;
And hope again, by fortune blest,
To spend an hour with you.
One hour with you, &c.

394 *High XII.*—BY ROB. MORRIS.

1 Here's Columns II. and Pillars V.
Support and grace our Halls of Truth,
But none such sparkling pleasures give,
As the Column that adorns the S.
"HIGH XII." the J. W. calls,
His Column grants the festive hour,
And through our antiquated Halls
Rich streams of social gladness pour.

2 'Tis then, all toil and care forgot,
The BOND indissoluble seems;
'Tis then the world's a happy spot,
And hope unmixed with sadness gleams:
HIGH XII.; I've shared the festive hour,
With those who realize the bliss,
And felt that life contains no more
Than sparkles in the joys of this.

3 What memories hover round the time!
What forms rise up to call it blest!
Departed friends — why should it dim
Our joy to know that they're at rest!
HIGH XII.; how they rejoiced to hear!
Quickly each implement laid down,
Glad to exchange for toil and care,
And heavy CROSS, a heavenly CROWN.

4 Then Comrades all, by 3 × 3,
Linked in the golden chain of truth,
A hearty welcome pledge with me
To the Column that adorns the S.
HIGH XII.: and never be the hour
Less free, less brotherly than now!
HIGH XII.; a rich libation pour
To joys that none but Masons know!

395 *The Emblems of the Craft.* R. MORRIS.

1 Who wears the SQUARE upon his breast,
Does in the eye of God attest,
And in the face of man,
That all his actions will compare
With the Divine, th' unerring Square,
That squares great Virtue's plan.—
That he erects his edifice
By *this design*, and *this*, and *this!* *

2 Who wears the LEVEL, says that pride
Does not within his soul abide,
Nor foolish vanity,—
That man has but a common doom,
And from his cradle to his tomb
One common destiny.
And he erects his edifice
By *this design*, and *this*, and *this!*

3 Who wears the G, ah, type divine!
Abhors the atmosphere of sin,
And trusts in God alone;
His father, Maker, friend he knows;—
He vows, and pays to God his vows
Before th' Eternal Throne.
And he erects his edifice
By *this design*, and *this*, and *this!*

4 Who wears the PLUMB, behold how true
His words, his walk! and could we view
The chambers of his soul;
Each thought enshrined, so pure, so good,
By the stern line of rectitude,
Points truly to the goal.
And he erects his edifice
By *this design*, and *this*, and *this!*

5 Thus life and beauty come to view,
In each design our fathers drew,
So glorious, so sublime!
Each breathes an odor from the bloom
Of gardens bright, beyond the tomb,—
Beyond the flight of time.
And bids us build on *this*, and *this*,
The walls of God's own edifice.

396 *Funeral Hymn.*—BY ROB. MORRIS.

1 Wreathe the mourning badge around—
Brothers pause! a funeral sound!
Where the parted had his home,
Meet and bear him to the tomb.

2 How his life-path has been trod,
Brothers, leave we unto God!
Friendship's mantle, love and faith,
Lend sweet fragrance e'en to death.

3 Here, amidst the things that sleep,
Let him rest—his grave is deep;
Death has triumphed, loving hands
Cannot raise him from his bands.

4 Dust to dust, the dark decree—
Soul to God, the soul is free:
Leave him with the lowly slain—
Brothers, we shall meet again.

* Illustration.

397 *Masonic Ode.* 7s. 6 lines.
BY REV. C. BABCOCK.

1 On thy bosom, mighty Lord,
  Gently may we fall asleep;
Trusting in thy sacred word,
  Keep us, Oh! our Father, keep:
From the terrors of the grave,
Save us, Judah's Lion, save!

2 As we pass the vale of death,
  Round us throw the arm of love;
When we yield this fleeting breath,
  Bear us to thy Lodge above,
In the "house not made with hands,"
Compassed round with angel bands.

3 In the resurrection morn,
  Raise us with thine own right hand;
Freed from envy and from scorn,
  Bring us to the better land —
Where from labor brethren cease,
Share refreshment—dwell in peace.

398 *Death of a Brother.* C. M.

1 As, bowed by sudden storms, the rose
  Sinks on the garden's breast,
Down to the grave our *brother* goes,
  In silence there to rest.

2 No more with us his tuneful voice
  The mystic hymn shall swell;
No more his cheerful heart rejoice,
  When peals the Sabbath bell.

3 But far away, in cloudless sphere,
  Amid a sinless throng,
He's joining, with celestial ear,
  The everlasting song.

4 No more we'll mourn our absent friend,
  But lift our earnest prayer,
That when our work of life shall end,
  We all may join him there.

399 *Ode.* C. P. M.
BY BRO. A. NICHOLS, JR.

1 Great Architect, supreme, divine,
  Whose wisdom planned the great design,
    And gave to nature birth;
Whose word with light adorned the skies,
Gave matter form, bade order rise,
    And blessed the new born earth.

2 O bless this love-cemented band,
  Formed and supported by thy hand,
    For Charity's employ;
To shield the wretched from despair,
To spread through scenes of grief and care,
    Reviving rays of joy.

3 The liberal arts by Thee designed,
  To polish, comfort, aid mankind,
    We labor to improve;
While we adore Jehovah's name,
Pour on our hearts the melting flame,
  And mould our hearts to love.

400 *Death of a Companion.* S. M.

1 Companion! thou hast gone!
  Rest from thy loved employ,—
The glorious victory thou-hast won,
  Enter thy Master's joy.

2 The pains of death are past;
  Labor and sorrow cease;
Life's pilgrimage is closed at last,
  The soul is found in peace.

3 Companion true, well done!
  Praise be thy new employ;
And while eternal ages run,
  Rest in thy Master's joy.

4 May we, who linger here,
  E'er true and faithful be;
Devoted in our humble sphere,
  Devoted, Lord, to Thee.

401 *Templar's Hymn.* 7s.
BY H. G. BARROWS.

1 To thy shrine, departed Lord,
  Come we, trusting in thy word;
In thy service, richly blest,
  Here, we pray thee let us rest.

2 Strong in Faith, in Hope, and Love,
  Lift we now our thoughts above;
To thy service, pure and free,
  Let us consecrated be.

3 Let thy light upon us shine,
  Fill our hearts with love divine;
On thy arm we trust our all,
  Keep us, that we never fall.

402 *Laying Corner Stone.* 7s. 6 lines
(BY BRO. ROB. MORRIS.)

1 Round the spot — Moriah's hill —
Mason's meet with cheerful will;
Him who stood as King that day,
We as cheerfully obey.
Lord, we love thy glorious Name,
Give the grace thou gavest him.

2 Round the spot thus chosen well,
Brothers, with fraternal hail,
Gather in your mystic ring,
Mystic words, and joyful sing.
Lord, our hearts, our souls are thine,
On our labors deign to shine.

3 Round the spot may Plenty reign,—
Peace, with spirit all benign;
Unity, the golden three —
Here their influence ever be.
Lord, these jewels of Thy store,
Send them bounteous, flowing o'er.

4 Round the spot where now we stand,
Soon will stand another band;
We to other worlds must go,
Called by Him we trust below.
Lord, thy spirit grant, that they
All thy counsel may obey.

Funeral Ceremonies.

No Freemason can be interred with the formalities of the Order, unless it be at his own request, or that of some of his family, (apprentices, foreigners and transient brethren excepted;) nor unless he has been advanced to the degree of Master Mason. From this rule there can be no *exception*. Fellow Crafts and Entered Apprentices are not entitled to Masonic Burial; nor to attend the Masonic processions on such occasions. (In some jurisdictions a Masonic Funeral Procession cannot be formed without a *Dispensation* from the constitutional authorities; in others, it is left with the Masters of the Subordinate Lodges.)

THE FUNERAL SERVICE.

The brethren being assembled at the Lodge room, or some other convenient place, the presiding officer opens the Lodge in the third degree, with the usual forms; and, having stated the purpose of the meeting, the service begins:—

MASTER. What man is he that liveth and shall not see death? Shall he deliver his soul from the hand of the grave?

RESPONSE. Man walketh in a vain shadow; he heapeth up riches, and cannot tell who shall gather them.

MASTER. When he dieth he shall carry nothing away; his glory shall not descend after him.

RESPONSE. Naked he came into the world, and naked he must return.

MASTER. The Lord gave, and the Lord hath taken away; blessed be the name of the Lord!

The Master then, taking the *roll* in his hand, says:—

Let us live and die like the righteous, that our last end may be like his!

RESPONSE. God is our God for ever and ever; he will be our guide even unto death!

The Master then records the name and age of the deceased upon the *roll,* and says:—

Almighty Father! in thy hands we leave, with humble submission, the soul of our deceased Brother.

The Brethren answer three times, giving the Grand Honors each time.

The will of God is accomplished! So mote it be. Amen.

The Master then deposits the *roll* in the archives, and repeats the following

PRAYER.

Most Glorious God! author of all good, and giver of all mercy! pour down thy blessing upon us, and strengthen our solemn engagements with the ties of sincere affection! May the present instance of mortality remind us of our approaching fate, and draw our attention toward Thee, the only refuge in time of need! that, when the awful moment shall arrive, that, when we are about to quit this transitory scene, the enlivening prospect of thy mercy may dispel the gloom of death; and, after our departure hence in peace, and in thy favor, may we be received into thine everlasting kingdom, to enjoy, in union with the souls of our departed friends, the just reward of a pious and virtuous life. Amen.

A procession is then formed, which moves to the house of the deceased, and from thence to the place of interment

ORDER OF PROCESSION AT A FUNERAL.

Tiler, with a drawn sword.
Stewards, with white rods.
Musicians,
[if they are Masons; otherwise they follow the Tiler.]
Master Masons.
Senior and Junior Deacons.
Marshal.   Secretary and Treasurer.
Senior and Junior Wardens.
Mark Masters.
Past Masters.
Royal Arch Masons.
Select Masters.
Knights Templars.
The Holy Writings,
[on a cushion covered with black cloth, carried by the oldest (or some suitable) member of the Lodge.]
The Master.
Clergy.

The Body, *COFFIN.* with the insignia placed thereon.
Pall Bearers.   Pall Bearers.

Chief Mourners.
Other Mourners.

When the procession arrives at the church-yard, the members of the Lodge form a circle around the grave, and the clergyman and officers of the Lodge take their station at the head of the grave, and the mourners at the foot. The procession *reverses* on arriving at the grave.

SERVICE AT THE GRAVE.

BRETHREN : — The solemn notes that betoken the dissolution of this earthly tabernacle, have again alarmed our outer door, and another spirit has been summoned to the land where our fathers have gone before us. Again we are called to assemble among the habitations of the dead, to behold the " narrow house appointed for all living." Here, around us, in that peace which the world cannot give, sleep the unnumbered dead. The gentle breeze fans their verdant covering — they heed it not; the sunshine and the storm pass over them, and they are not disturbed ; stones and lettered monuments symbolize the affection of surviving friends, yet no sound proceeds from them, save that silent but thrilling admonition — " seek ye the narrow path and the strait gate that lead unto eternal life." We are again called upon to consider the uncertainty of human life ; the immutable certainty of death, and the vanity of all human pursuits. Decrepitude and decay are written upon every living thing. The cradle and the coffin stand in juxtaposition to each other ; and it is a melancholy truth, that so soon as we begin to live, that moment also we begin to die. It is passing strange, that, notwithstanding the daily mementos of mortality that cross our path ; notwithstanding the funeral bell so often tolls in our ears, and the " mournful processions " go about our streets, that we will not more seriously consider our approaching fate. We go on from design to design, add hope to hope, and lay out plans for the employment of many years, until we are suddenly alarmed at the approach of the Messenger of Death, at a moment when we least expect him, and which we probably conclude to be the meridian of our existence.

What, then, are all the externals of human dignity, the power of wealth, the dreams of ambition, the pride of intellect, or the charms of beauty, when Nature has paid her just debt ? Fix your eyes on the last sad scene, and view life stript of its ornaments, and exposed in its natural meanness, and you must be persuaded of the utter emptiness of these delusions. In the grave all fallacies are detected, all ranks are levelled, and all distinctions are done away.

While we drop the sympathetic tear over the grave of our deceased brother, let us cast around his foibles, whatever they may have been, the *broad mantle of Masonic charity*, nor withhold from his memory the commendation that his virtues claim at our hands. Perfection on earth has never yet been attained ; the wisest as well as the best of men have gone astray. Suffer, then, the apologies of human nature to plead for him who can no longer extenuate for himself.

Our present meeting and proceedings will have been vain and useless, if they fail to excite our serious reflections, and strengthen our resolutions of amendment. Be then persuaded, my brethren, by the uncertainty of human life, and the unsubstantial nature of all its pursuits, and no longer postpone the all-important concern of preparing for eternity. Let us each embrace the present moment, and while time and opportunity offer prepare for that great change, when the pleasures of the world shall be as poison to our lips, and happy reflections of a well spent life afford the only consolation. Thus shall our hopes be not frustrated, nor we hurried, unprepared, into the presence of that all-wise and powerful Judge, to whom the secrets of every heart are known. Let us resolve to maintain, with greater assiduity, the dignified character of our profession. May our *faith* be evinced in a correct moral walk and deportment ; may our *hope* be bright as the glorious mysteries that will be revealed hereafter ; and our *charity* boundless as the wants of our fellow creatures. And having faithfully discharged the great duties which we owe to God, to our neighbor, and ourselves ; when at last it shall please the Grand Master of the universe to summon us into his eternal presence, may the *trestle-board* of our whole lives pass such inspection that it may be given unto each of us to " eat of the hidden manna," and to receive the " white stone with a new name written," that will insure perpetual and unspeakable happiness at his right hand.

The Master then presenting the Apron, continues:

The lamb-skin, or white apron, is the emblem of innocence, and the badge of a Mason. It is more ancient than the golden fleece or Roman eagle ; more honorable than the star and garter, when worthily worn.

The Master then deposits it in the grave:

This emblem I now deposit in the grave of our deceased brother. By it we are reminded of the universal dominion of Death. The arm of Friendship cannot interpose to prevent his coming ; the wealth of the world cannot purchase our release ; nor will the innocence of youth, or the charms of beauty, propitiate his purpose. The mattock, the coffin, and the melancholy grave, admonish us of our mortality, and that, sooner or later, these frail bodies must moulder in their parent dust.

The Master, holding the *evergreen*, continues:

This *evergreen*, which once marked the temporary resting-place of the illustrious dead, is an emblem of our faith in the immortality of the soul. By this, we are reminded that we have an immortal part within us, that shall survive the grave, and which shall never, never, never die. By it we are admonished, that, though like our brother, whose remains lie before us, we shall soon be clothed in the habiliments of Death, and deposited in the silent tomb, yet, through the merits of a divine and ascended Saviour, we may confidently hope that our souls will bloom in eternal spring.

The brethren then move in procession round the place of interment, and severally drop the sprig of evergreen into the grave; after which, the public Grand Honors are given. (See Mackey's Lexicon.) The Master then continues:

From time immemorial, it has been the custom among the fraternity of Free and Accepted Masons, at the request of a brother, to accompany his corpse to the place of interment, and there to deposit his remains with the usual formalities.

In conformity to this usage, and at the request of our deceased brother, whose memory we revere, and whose loss we now deplore, we have assembled in the character of Masons, to offer up to his memory, before the world, the last tribute of our affection; thereby demonstrating the sincerity of our past esteem for him, and our steady attachment to the principles of the Order.

The great Creator having been pleased, out of his infinite mercy, to remove our brother from the cares and troubles of this transitory existence to a state of endless duration, thus severing another link from the fraternal chain that binds us together; may we, who survive him, be more strongly cemented in the ties of union and friendship; that, during the short space allotted us here, we may wisely and usefully employ our time; and, in the reciprocal intercourse of kind and friendly acts, mutually promote the welfare and happiness of each other. Unto the grave we have consigned the body of our deceased brother; earth to earth, ashes to ashes, dust to dust; there to remain until the trump shall sound on the resurrection morn. We can cheerfully leave him in the hands of a Being who has done all things well; who is glorious in holiness, fearful in praises, doing wonders.

To those of his immediate relatives and friends, who are most heart-stricken at the loss we have all sustained, we have but little of this world's consolation to offer. We can sincerely, deeply, and most affectionately sympathize with them in their afflictive bereavement. But in the beautiful spirit of the Christian's theology, we dare to say, that He, who "tempers the wind to the shorn lamb," looks down with infinite compassion upon the widow and fatherless, in the hour of their desolation; and that the same benevolent Saviour, who wept while on earth, will fold the arms of his love and protection around those who put their trust in Him.

Then let us improve this solemn warning, that at last, when the "sheeted dead" are stirring, when the "great white throne" is set, we shall receive from the omniscient Judge, the thrilling invitation, "Come, ye blessed of my Father, inherit the kingdom prepared for you from the foundation of the world."

RESPONSE. So mote it be. Amen.

The following, or some other suitable Hymn may be sung:

FUNERAL HYMN.

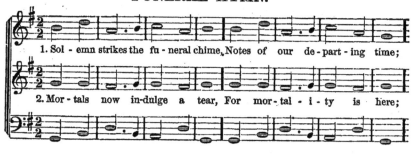

1. Sol - emn strikes the fu - neral chime, Notes of our de - part - ing time;

2. Mor - tals now in - dulge a tear, For mor - tal - i - ty is here;

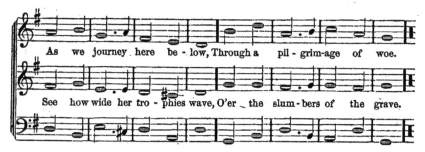

As we journey here be - low, Through a pil - grim-age of woe.

See how wide her tro - phies wave, O'er the slum - bers of the grave.

3 Here another guest we bring,
  Seraphs, of celestial wing,
  To our fun'ral altar come,
  Waft a friend and Brother home.

4 Lord of all below, above,
  Fill our souls with Truth and Love;
  As dissolves our earthly tie,
  Take us to thy Lodge on High.

The two first verses may be sung on entering the Graveyard, while moving in procession; and the third and last verses during the ceremonies at the grave.

The service at the Grave concludes with the following, or some suitable Prayer:

PRAYER.

Almighty and most merciful Father, we adore thee as the God of time and of eternity. As it has pleased thee to take from the light of our abode, one dear to our hearts, we beseech thee to bless and sanctify unto us this dispensation of thy Providence. Inspire our hearts with wisdom from on high, that we may glorify thee in all our ways. May we realize that thine All-seeing Eye is upon us, and be influenced by the spirit of truth and love to perfect obedience—that we may enjoy the divine approbation here below. And when our toils on earth shall have ceased, may be raised to the enjoyment of fadeless light and immortal life in that kingdom where faith and hope shall end—and love and joy prevail through eternal ages. And thine, O righteous Father, shall be the glory forever. Amen.

RESPONSE. So mote it be. Amen.

BURIAL SERVICE
OF THE
Orders of Masonic Knighthood.*

GENERAL REGULATIONS.

1. No Sir Knight can be buried with the funeral honors of Knighthood, unless he be a Knight Templar in regular standing.

2. It shall be the duty of the E. Commander to convene the Sir Knights of the Commandery, upon notice of the death of a Sir Knight who may be entitled to receive funeral honors, upon request made when living, or by his family after his decease, for the purpose of attending the funeral ceremonies.

3. Sir Knights, on such occasions, will attend in full uniform, pursuant to the regulations; their sword-hilts and the banner of the Commandery being suitably dressed in mourning.

4. On the coffin of the deceased Sir Knight will be placed his hat and sword; and, if an officer, his jewel, trimmed with crape.

5. The E. Commander will preside during the services, and, assisted by the Prelate, lead in the ceremonies, pursuant to the Ritual. If Grand Officers or Past Grand Officers be present, they will be allotted a place in the procession according to their rank; and if the Grand Prelate, or a Past Grand Prelate be present, he will take the place of the Prelate.

6. The Sir Knights will assemble at their Asylum, and march to the residence of the deceased in the usual order of processions; the line being headed by the Warder, and the Officers being in the rear, according to rank; that is, the E. Commander last; the Prelate being preceded by the Holy Writings, carried on a cushion, and the arms and hat of the deceased borne in the rear of the E. Commander. On arriving at the house, the lines are opened, and the E. Commander passes to the front and receives the body, placing the hat and sword on the coffin, as above directed.

7. The procession is then formed as before; the body, with the mourners and citizens present, being in the rear of the Sir Knights, and in front of the officers. If the services are performed at a church or place of public worship, the procession, on arriving, will enter in reversed order, the E. Commander and Prelate with the other officers preceding the body and mourners.

8. When the public or religious services are concluded, the face of the deceased will be uncovered, and the Sir Knights (or a detachment of them,) will form the "cross of steel," over the body, the E. Commander, with the Prelate, being at the head of the coffin, and the other officers at the foot.

9. When more convenient or desirable, the part of the service before going to the grave, as here indicated, may be performed at the house of the deceased, or be deferred till at the grave.

THE FUNERAL SERVICE OF KNIGHTHOOD WILL BE CONDUCTED
ACCORDING TO THE FOLLOWING

Ritual:

E. COMMANDER. Sir Knights: In the solemn rites of our Order we have often been reminded of the great truth, that we were born to die. Mortality has been

---

* This beautiful Burial Service was prepared by M. E. Jno. L. Lewis, Jr., at the request of the Grand Commandery of New York.

brought to view, that we might more earnestly seek an immortality beyond this fleeting life, where death can come no more for ever. The sad and mournful funeral knell has betokened that another spirit has winged its flight to a new state of existence. An alarm has come to the door of our Asylum, and the messenger was Death, and none presumed to say to the awful presence:—"Who dare approach?" A pilgrim warrior has been summoned, and "there is no discharge in that war." A burning taper of life, in our Commandery, has been extinguished, and none, save the High and Holy One, can relight it. All that remains of our beloved Companion Sir Knight lies mute before us, and the light of the eye, and the breathing of the lips, in their language of fraternal greeting, have ceased for us, forever, on this side of the grave. His sword, vowed only to be drawn in the cause of truth, justice, and rational liberty, reposes still in its scabbard, and our arms can no more shield him from wrong or oppression.

The Sir Knights here return arms.

It is meet at such a time that we should be silent, and let the words of the Infinite and Undying speak, that we may gather consolation from His revelations, and impress upon our minds lessons of wisdom and instruction, and the meetness of preparation for the last great change which must pass upon us all.

Let us be reverently attentive while Sir Knight, our Prelate, reads to us a lesson from the Holy Scriptures.

PRELATE. Help, Lord! for the faithful fail from among the children of men.

RESPONSE. Help us, oh Lord!

PRELATE. The righteous cry, and the Lord heareth, and delivereth them out of all their troubles.

RESPONSE. Hear us, oh Lord!

PRELATE. The Lord is nigh unto them that are of a broken heart; and saveth such as be of a contrite spirit.

RESPONSE. Be nigh unto us, oh Lord!

PRELATE. The Lord redeemeth the souls of his servants; and none of them that trust in him shall be desolate.

RESPONSE. Redeem us, oh Lord!

PRELATE. For I will not trust in my bow, neither shall my sword save me.

RESPONSE. Redeem us, oh Lord!

PRELATE. But God will redeem my soul from the power of the grave; for he shall receive me.

RESPONSE. Redeem us, oh Lord!

PRELATE. Wilt thou show wonders to the dead? shall the dead arise and praise thee? Shall thy loving kindness be declared in the grave? or thy faithfulness in destruction?

RESPONSE. Save us, oh Lord!

PRELATE. We spend our years as a tale that is told. The days of our years are threescore years and ten; and if by reason of strength they be fourscore years, yet is their strength, labor, and sorrow; for it is soon cut off, and we fly away. So teach us to number our days, that we may apply our hearts unto wisdom.

RESPONSE. Teach us, oh Lord!

PRELATE. For he knoweth our frame; he remembereth that we are dust. As for man, his days are as grass; as a flower of the field he flourisheth. For the wind passeth over it, and it is gone; and the place thereof shall know it no more. But the mercy of the Lord is from everlasting to everlasting, upon them that fear him.

RESPONSE. Show mercy, oh Lord!

PRELATE. We shall not all sleep, but we shall all be changed; in a moment, in the twinkling of an eye, at the last trump; for the trumpet shall sound, and the dead shall be raised incorruptible, and we shall be changed. For this corruptible must put on incorruption, and this mortal must put on immortality. So when this corruptible shall have put on incorruption, and this mortal shall have put on immortality, then shall be brought to pass the saying that is written,— Death is swallowed up in victory. O death, where is thy sting? O grave, where is thy victory?

RESPONSE. O death, where is thy sting! O grave, where is thy victory!

PRELATE. The sting of death is sin; and the strength of sin is the law. But thanks be to God, which giveth us the victory through our Lord Jesus Christ.

RESPONSE. Thanks be to God!

E. COMMANDER. Shall the memory of our departed brother fade from among men?

RESPONSE. It is cherished in our soul forever!

E. COMMANDER. Shall no record be left of his virtues and worth?

RESPONSE. It is inscribed upon our hearts; it is written in our archives; the heart may cease to throb, and the archives may moulder and decay; but the tablets of the Recording Angel on high can never perish.

The Recorder here opens the Book of Records of the Commandery, on which a page is set apart, suitably inscribed, and says:

Thus it is written

The Sir Knights uncover, and bow their heads.

E. COMMANDER. He was a true and courteous knight, and has fallen in life's struggle full knightly with his armor on, prepared for knightly deeds.

PRELATE. Rest to his ashes, and peace to his soul!

RESPONSE. Rest to his ashes, and peace to his soul!

PRELATE. Sovereign Ruler of the Universe! into thy hands we devoutly and submissively commit the departed spirit.

RESPONSE. Thy will be done, oh God!

THE FOLLOWING HYMN WILL BE SUNG.

Words by Rob. MORRIS, K. T.

Arranged by J. B. TAYLOR, K. T.

1. Pre - cious in the sight of Hea - ven, Is the scene where Christians die;
2. Here a - bove our broth-er weep-ing, Thro' our tears we seize this hope,
3. Knights of Christ! your ranks are bro-ken! Close your front, the Foe is nigh!

Souls, with all their sins for - giv - en, To the courts of glo - ry fly;
He in Je - sus sweet - ly sleep - ing, Shall a - wake to glo - ry up.
Shield to shield, be - hold the To - ken, As he saw it in the sky!

Ev - 'ry sor - row, ev - 'ry bur - den, Ev - 'ry cross they lay it down.
He has borne his cross in sor - row, Wea - ry pil - grim all for - lorn,
By this Sign, so bright, so glo - rious, You shall Conquer! if you strive,

Je - sus gives them rich - est guer-don, In his own im - mor - tal crown.
When the sun shines bright to - mor-row, 'Twill re - veal his sparkling crown.
And like him, tho' dead, vic - to - rious In the sight of Je - sus live.

The following PRAYER will then be made by the Prelate; (or an extemporaneous Prayer may be made by him, or by any Clergyman present, as may be preferred.)

FATHER OF LIGHTS! in this dark and trying hour of calamity and sorrow, we humbly lift our hearts to Thee. Give us, we pray, that light which cometh down from above. Thou hast mercifully said, in Thy holy word, that the bruised reed Thou wouldst not break; remember in mercy, oh Lord, before Thee. [Be Thou, at this hour, the Father of the fatherless, and the widow's God. Administer to them the consolations which they so sorely need.] Cause us to look away from these sad scenes of frail mortality, to the hopes which lie beyond the grave, and bind us yet closer together in the ties of brotherly love and affection. While we see how frail is man, and how uncertain the continuance of our lives upon the earth, and are reminded of our own mortality, lead us by Thy grace and spirit to turn our thoughts to those things which make for our everlasting peace; and give us a frame of mind to make a proper improvement of all the admonitions of Thy providence, and fix our thoughts more devotedly on Thee, the only sure refuge in time of need. And at last, when our earthly pilgrimage shall be ended, "when the silver cord shall be loosed, and the golden bowl be broken," oh wilt Thou, in that moment of mortal extremity, be indeed *Immanuel* — Christ with us; may "the lamp of Thy love" dispel the gloom of the dark valley, and we be enabled, by the commendations of Thy Son, to gain admission into the blessed Asylum above; and, in Thy glorious presence, amidst its ineffable mysteries, enjoy a union with the spirits of the departed, perfect as is the happiness of heaven, and durable as the eternity of God. *Amen!*

RESPONSE. Amen, and Amen and Amen!

The procession will then form, and march to the place of interment in the same order as before.

On arriving at the place, while forming in order, a suitable Dirge, or the following Hymn may be sung:

AIR — PLEYEL'S HYMN.　　　　Arranged by J. B. TAYLOR.

1. Soft - ly, sad - ly, bear him forth To his dark and si - lent bed;

2. By our tri - als, hope, and fear; By our an - guish keen-ly felt;

3. This, our broth - er, gone be - fore, May we in re-mem-brance keep,

Weep not that he's lost to earth, Weep not that his spir-it's fled.

Let us trust God will be near, When we're at His al-tar knelt.

Hop-ing, as time pass-es o'er, We shall meet where none e'er weep.

4 Sadly now we leave his form,
  In the tomb to moulder still;
  Hoping in th' eternal morn,
  Christ his promise will fulfil.

5 One last look—one parting sigh;
  Ah, too sad for words to tell;
  Yet! though tears now dim each eye,
  Hope we still, and sigh, farewell!

On reaching the grave, the Sir Knights will form a triangle around it, the base being at the foot, the E. Commander and Prelate being at the head of the grave, and the friends and relatives at the foot, and the services will thus proceed:

PRELATE. Sir Knights: There is one sacred spot upon the earth where the foot-falls of our march are unheeded; our trumpets quicken no pulse, and incite no fear; the rustling of our banners and the gleam of our swords awaken no emotion— it is the silent city of the dead, where we now stand. Awe rests upon every heart, and the stern warrior's eyes are bedewed with feelings which never shame his manhood. It needs no siege, nor assault, nor beleaguering host, to enter its walls; we fear no sortie, and listen for no battle-shout. No Warder's challenge greets the ear, nor do we wait awhile with patience for permission to enter.

Hither must we all come at last; and the stoutest heart and the manliest form that surrounds me will then be led a captive, without title or rank, in the chains of mortality and the habiliments of slavery, to the King of Terrors.

But if he has been faithful to the Captain of his salvation, a true soldier of the Cross; if he has offered suitable gifts at the shrine of his departed Lord, and bears the signet of the Lion of the tribe of Judah, then may he claim to be of that princely house, and to be admitted to audience with the Sovereign Master of Heaven and Earth. Then will he be stripped of the chains of earthly captivity, and clothed in a white garment, glistening as the sun, and be seated with princes and rulers, and partake of a libation, not of death and sorrow, but of that wine which is drank forever new in the Father's kingdom above.

We cannot come here without subdued hearts and softened affections. Often, as the challenge comes which takes from our side some loved associate, some cherished companion in arms, and often as the trumpet sounds its wailing notes to summon us to the death-bed, and to the brink of the sepulchre, we cannot contemplate "the last of earth" unmoved. Each successive death-note snaps some fibre which binds us to this lower existence, and makes us pause and reflect upon that dark and gloomy chamber where we must all terminate our pilgrimage. Well will it be for our peace then, if we can wash our hands, not only in token of sincerity, but of every guilty stain, and give honest and satisfactory answers to the questions required.

The sad and solemn scene, now before us, stirs up these recollections with a force and vivid power which we have hitherto unfelt. He who now slumbers in that last, long, unbroken sleep of death, was our brother. With him have we walked the pilgrimage of life, and kept watch and ward together in its vicissitudes and trials. He is now removed beyond the effect of our praise or censure. That we loved him, our presence here evinces, and we remember him in scenes to which the world was not witness, and where the better feelings of humanity were exhibited without disguise. That he had faults and foibles, is but to repeat what his mortality demonstrates — that he had a human nature not divine. Over those errors, whatever they may have been, we cast, while living, the mantle of charity; it should, with much more reason, enshroud him in death. We, who have been taught to extend the point of charity, even to a foe, when fallen, cannot be severe or merciless toward a loved brother.

The memory of his virtues lingers in our remembrance, and reflects its shining lustre beyond the portals of the tomb. The earthern vase, which has contained precious odors, will lose none of its fragrance though the clay be broken and shattered. So be it with our brother's memory.

The Junior Warden then removes the sword and hat from the coffin, which last will then be lowered into the grave, while the Prelate repeats as follows:

PRELATE. "I am the resurrection and the life: he that believeth in me, though he were dead, yet shall he live; and whosoever liveth, and believeth in me, shall never die." To the earth we commit the mortal remains of our deceased brother, as we have already commended his soul to his Creator, with humble submission to Divine Providence. (*Here cast some earth on the coffin.*) Earth to earth; (*here cast again,*) ashes to ashes; (*here cast more earth,*) dust to dust; till the morn of the resurrection, when, like our arisen and ascended Redeemer, he will break the bands of death, and abide the judgment of the great day. Till then, friend, brother, Sir Knight, farewell! Light be the ashes upon thee, and "may the sunshine of Heaven beam bright on thy waking!"

RESPONSE. Amen, and Amen and Amen!

The Junior Warden then presents the sword to the E. Commander, who says:

E. COMMANDER. Our departed brother Sir Knight was taught, while living, that this sword, in his hands, as a true and courteous Knight, was endowed with three most estimable qualities: its hilt with *fortitude* undaunted; its blade with *justice* impartial; and its point with *mercy* unrestrained. To this lesson, with its deep emblematical significance, we trust he gave wise heed. He could never grasp it without being reminded of the lively significance of the attributes it inculcated. He has borne the pangs of dissolving nature — may we trust that it was with the same *fortitude* that he sustained the trials of this passing existence; to his name and memory be *justice* done, as we hope to receive the like meed ourselves; and may that *mercy*, unrestrained, which is the glorious attribute of the Son of God; interpose in his behalf to blunt the sword of divine justice, and admit him to the blessed companionship of saints and angels in the realms of light and life eternal!

RESPONSE. Amen, and Amen, and Amen!

The Senior Warden then presents a Cross to the Prelate, who says:

PRELATE. This symbol of faith — the Christian's hope, and the Christian's trust — we again place upon the breast of our brother, there to remain till the last trumpet shall sound, and earth and sea yield up their dead. Though it may, in the past history of our race, have been perverted at times into an ensign of oppression, and crime, and wrong; though it may have been made the emblem of fraud, and superstition, and moral darkness, yet its significance still remains as the badge of a Christian warrior. It calls to mind Gethsemane and its sorrowful garden; the judgment-hall of Pilate, and the pitiless crown of thorns; Golgotha and Calvary, and their untold agonies, that fallen man might live and inherit everlasting life. If an inspired Apostle was not ashamed of the Cross, neither should we be; if he gloried in the significance of the truths it shadowed forth, so ought we to rejoice in it as the speaking witness of our reliance beyond the grave. May this hope of the living have been the anchor to the soul of our departed brother — the token to admit him to that peaceful haven "where the wicked cease from troubling, and the weary are at rest."

RESPONSE. Amen, and Amen, and Amen!

The Prelate then casts the Cross into the grave, and continues:

PRELATE. The orders of Christian Knighthood were instituted in a dark period of the world's history, but their mission was high and holy. To succor and protect the sorrowing and destitute, the innocent and oppressed, was their vow and their life-long labor and duty. For long, long years, they well and nobly performed their vows, and did their devoirs. In those rude ages the steel blade was oftener the arbiter of justice, than the judgments of judicial tribunals, or the decrees of magistrates. So long as the Templars adhered to their vows of poverty, they were virtuous and innocent, and their language was, in truth, " Silver and gold have I none, but such as I have, give I unto thee." But, with the accession of wealth and civil power, they were tempted and fell from their high estate, and their possessions attracted the cupidity, and their prowess incurred the hatred of the despots of those times. When the martyred De Molay had perished, and the Order was proscribed, they united with the fraternity of Free and Accepted Masons, and returned to their primitive simplicity of manners; and a rough habit, coarse diet, and severe duty, was all that was offered to their votaries.

In our land we have perpetuated only the distinctive rites, with the appellations and regulations of the defenders of the Holy Sepulchre — the early champions and soldiers of the Cross — and this as a guerdon of merit, not a badge of rank. The sword, in our hands, is more as a symbol of the duties we are vowed to fulfil, than as an instrument of assault or defence. We claim to exercise practical virtues in the holy bonds of our confraternity, in humble imitation of those renowned knights of the olden time; for there is still, in this refined age, innocence to be guarded, widowed hearts to be relieved of their burdens, and orphanage to be protected from the chill blasts of a wintry world. And to be true and courteous is not limited to any age or clime.

Our brother, whose cold and lifeless remains have just been committed to the earth, was one of our fraternal band, bound by the same ties and pledged to the same duties. To his bereaved and mourning friends and relatives, we have but little of worldly consolation to offer, but we do tender to them our heart-felt sympathies. And if the solemn and interesting ceremonies, in which we have been engaged, have not pointed to them a higher hope and a better consolation, then all our condolences would be in vain.

Sir Knight companions, let us pray :

ALMIGHTY and most merciful God! we adore Thee as the Sovereign Ruler of all events, both in time and for eternity. As it hath pleased thee to take from our ranks one dear to our hearts, we beseech thee to bless and sanctify unto us this dispensation of Thy providence. Inspire our hearts with wisdom from on high, that we may glorify Thee in all our ways. May we have Thy divine assistance, oh, most merciful God! to redeem our misspent time ; and in the discharge of the important duties Thou hast assigned us in our moral warfare here below, may we be guided by faith and humility, courage and constancy, to perform our allotted pilgrimage acceptable in Thy sight, without asking a remission of years from Thee. And when our career on earth is finished; and the sepulchre appointed for all the living receives our mortal bodies, may our souls, disengaged from their cumbrous dust, flourish and bloom in eternal day, and enjoy that rest which Thou hast prepared for Thy good and faithful servants in Thy blessed Asylum of peace beyond the vails of earth. All which we ask through the mediation of our Redeemer, King of kings, and Lord of lords. *Amen!*

RESPONSE. Amen, and Amen, and Amen!

E. COMMANDER. Attention, Sir Knights:

The lines are then formed, and the Cross of steel made over the grave, and the following HYMN is sung:

Air.—WILMOT.

Arranged by J. B. TAYLOR.

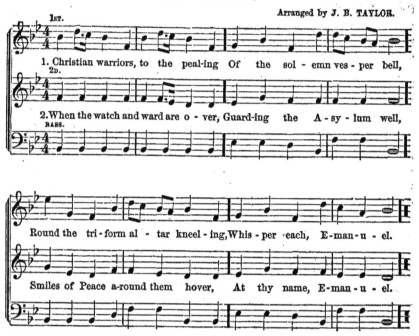

1. Christian warriors, to the peal-ing Of the sol - emn ves - per bell,
2. When the watch and ward are o - ver, Guard-ing the A - sy - lum well,

Round the tri-form al - tar kneel-ing, Whis - per each, E-man-u - el.

Smiles of Peace a-round them hover, At thy name, E-man-u - el.

3
When the matin-notes are ringing,
Cheerfully from mount and dell,
Strength for warfare still is springing
From Thy name, Emanuel.

4
When some deed of empire sharing,
Deeds like those traditions tell,
Prompts each Knight to noble daring,
'Tis for Thee, Emanuel.

5
When the storm-clouds darkly lower
On our pathway dark and fell,
Knights heroic will not cower,
Cheered by Thee, Emanuel.

6
When death's fearful damps are stealing,
And is breathed the last "Farewell!"
All the brighter world revealing,
Thou shalt come, Emanuel!

The Sir Knights may then escort the friends of the deceased to their home, or return to their Asylum, as may be expedient.

A. B. KIDDER'S MUSIC TYPOGRAPHY, BOSTON.

A LITTLE SECRET

ANN EVANS | JAMES LAWRENCE

"Its glassy eyes stared blindly."

A Little Secret ISBN 978-1-78837-221-3

Publisher: Susan Ross
Senior Editor: Danny Pearson
Editorial Coordinator: Claire Morgan
Copyeditor: Cheryl Lanyon
Designer: Bigtop Design Ltd
Illustration: James Lawrence

2 4 6 8 10 9 7 5 3

CHAPTER 1
THE VISIT

"No one's making you come," I said, looking at my girlfriend's moody face.

"But it's every Sunday, Lucas!" Kay moaned. "And what's the point? She doesn't know you. She doesn't even know what planet she's on!"

That was true. My great gran, Granny-May, as I'd always called her even though her name was Mabel, thought she was a little kid again. A five-year-old rather than almost ninety. But I still liked to visit her now and then.

I tried to explain to Kay. "OK, so she's old and her head is all mixed up. But she still likes visitors."

I stood in Kay's doorway, waiting for her to make up her mind. We'd been seeing each other for four months now. And even though she was sometimes a bit moody, I liked her — a lot!

She flashed those beautiful eyes at me, trying to get her own way. "Lucas, I hate that care home, it's boring and full of smelly old people."

"You'll be old and smelly one day," I said, then winked. "Actually…"

She dived on me, prodding, poking, her long black hair swishing. "Cheek! I don't smell!"

"Only of roses!" I told her, laughing, liking the feel of her hands all over me. Even though some of those jabs hurt. Fending her off, I said, "Anyway, I'm going to see my great gran. Come if you want."

"Boring!" she sighed, but grabbed her keys and followed me out.

The Oaks Care Home wasn't far, just a twenty-minute walk. And Kay was right, it did smell. But it had nice staff and a cheery lounge where the old people sat around drinking tea. Granny-May was asleep in a chair.

"Granny-May…" I touched her old, wrinkled hand. Her hair was pure white. Her skin like old pastry.

"Wh…?" Her pale, watery eyes blinked open. Then, peering at me she said, puzzled, "Terry? Terry, is that you?"

"No, Granny-May, it's me, Lucas."

She frowned. "Lucas? Where's Terry?"

I pulled up a chair. Kay stood, arms folded. "Terry will be back soon," I said. There was no point in asking who Terry was — her brother maybe.

"He'll be late. He needs to hurry up."

"I'm sure he'll be here soon," I said, then nodded to where Kay stood, still looking grumpy. "Look Granny-May, Kay's come to see you. My girlfriend. Do you remember Kay?"

Kay groaned. "You won't get any sense out of her!"

"Shush! She's not deaf, you know."

"Daft, more like," Kay muttered under her breath.

Granny-May smiled, but not at Kay. I don't think she'd even noticed her. But it was a big, wide smile, making her false teeth wobble. She was excited, like a kid. "We're having a party. Susan is ten today."

"That's nice. Is Susan your friend?" I asked.

"No, silly! Susan is my big sister."

OK, so she was stuck in the past. But these were real memories from long ago. Her memories.

Kay cut in, a bit unkindly. "So your sister is ten, and she's your big sister. So what does that make you then?"

I cast Kay a look, telling her to *just leave it.*

She hates being told what to do. But she clamped her mouth shut, then flicked her hair in a way that warned me she was not a happy bunny. Looking bored stiff, she gazed blankly across the room.

"Are you coming to the party?" Granny-May asked me.

"We'd love to!" I held Granny-May's frail, bony hand and let her talk.

Sometimes she said interesting stuff. Like when she thought the war was going on and we were in an air-raid shelter. In her head we were really there. She told me how it felt, how it smelled, the noise of the bombs dropping, everything. And that had proved really useful for my schoolwork. Got me top marks for an essay I had to do on Britain in the war.

Sometimes she talked about her family. She'd lived in the same house all her life, right up until they'd put her in this care home. Mum and Dad had the keys to her house now. They'd have to sell it before long. Granny-May wouldn't be going home.

"Has your mother made a birthday cake?" I asked, when Granny-May looked ready to nod back off to sleep.

Her pale eyes lit up. Her voice became shrill, like a child's. "Oh yes! And jelly. Mama showed me how to make jelly. Shall I show you?"

Behind me, Kay muttered, "Someone tell her she's eighty-five, not five!"

"Shush!" I hissed. "No point. Just go with the flow."

My great gran leaned towards me. She put a finger to her lips. "I have a little secret."

"Have you?" I said, just as softly. "What is it? Can you tell me?"

"Bella not come to the party." She spoke like a child.

I had no idea who Bella was. "Won't she? Why not?"

Her voice got even softer. Her watery eyes shifted left and right. "Because…"

"Yes?"

"Bella in the wardrobe. Bella…" she tapped her head with her finger, then moved it in circles. "Papa says Bella not right in the head."

"Who's Bella?" Kay blurted out.

Granny-May looked up at Kay and frowned. "Bella bad girl!"

"Yes, well, I gather that," said Kay harshly, "or she wouldn't be locked up in the wardrobe."

Kay stepped closer to Granny-May. The closest she'd ever been to her. Then before I could stop her, she said loudly and slowly, "Who… is… Bella?"

Granny-May's red-rimmed eyes fixed on Kay. Her voice suddenly hard. "She my bad sister. She locked up in wardrobe now. She not going to the party. Bella not going anywhere… NEVER!"

Her last word came out as a screech. Kay jumped a mile.

It served her right, really. It wasn't a nice way to talk to an old lady.

A nurse came rushing over. "Now, now, Mabel dear, what's all this shouting?"

Granny-May looked suddenly like a sullen child. She put her thumb in her mouth and sat rocking back and forth in her chair.

"I think she's a bit tired. I'll get her a cup of tea," the nurse said, looking at me and Kay. "Cup of tea, Mabel dear?"

I took the hint — time to go. And Kay had obviously had enough for one day.

"We'll be off then." I patted my great gran's hand. "See you soon, Granny-May."

She didn't answer. Didn't look up. She just sat in her chair, rocking back and forth, lost in her memories.

Outside, Kay glared at me. "She gets worse! And who's poor old Bella, locked up in a wardrobe? I hope they let her out — a hundred years ago."

I'd never known my great gran raise her voice. That was odd. And like Kay said, who on Earth was Bella? Her bad sister? That was a bit worrying.

"Well, speak to me, then!" shouted Kay.

I'd been miles away. "Oh, sorry."

Kay slipped her arm through mine, which was nice. Showed she'd forgiven me for dragging her along — phew!

"What was the crazy old biddy on about?" she went on. "Did she even have any brothers and sisters?"

"Yeah, Mum says she was one of about six kids," I said. "There were twins in the family too… I think."

"Is she the last one alive?"

I shrugged. "As far as I know."

Kay raised her eyebrows. "Unless there's still one locked in the wardrobe!"

CHAPTER 2
LOCKED AWAY

I knew where my parents kept Granny-May's house keys. I guessed it would be OK to grab them. I knew it was stupid. It was just a confused old lady's ramblings, but I needed to check.

Maybe, long ago, Bella was bad. Maybe she did get locked in the wardrobe for being naughty. Maybe that was the old-fashioned *naughty step*.

Kay was dead keen on checking out Granny-May's house too. She needed no persuading even though it was a half-an-hour walk.

Granny-May's was a big old Victorian house, three storeys high. Kay looked up at it and her jaw dropped. "Oh, wow!"

We went up the stone steps and I turned the key. There was lots of post on the floor. I sorted it into two piles: junk and stuff for Mum to deal with. Kay went off to look about.

There was an eerie silence in the house now, just the creaking of floorboards. Yet once it must have been alive with chatter and laughter.

All Granny-May's things were just as she'd left them. Deep, high-backed chairs; big old vases; an antique clock no longer ticking.

"It's so old fashioned!" Kay said, poking through drawers and cupboards. "Some of these antiques will be worth a fortune."

It didn't seem right, her prying into my great gran's things. But at least she was showing an interest.

"We need to go upstairs. Check out the wardrobe."

She came running after me. "Wait for me!"

There were wardrobes in every bedroom. Big, heavy, oak wardrobes. Every one full of clothes, shoes and boxes. Just normal stuff.

I laughed at my stupid imagination. Don't know what I'd expected to find really. But, happily, there was no *bad sister* locked away.

I was getting bored, but Kay was loving it. She sure did have a nosy streak! She was digging deep into every wardrobe, opening bags and boxes.

"Found some old photos!"

She passed me a tin full of old black-and-white prints. "These are cool," I said. "I'll take them home. Mum and Dad are going to love them!"

Kay carried on her searching, or should I say being nosy?

"Lucas, you'll make a fortune on eBay with all this stuff — whoops!" She was on her knees, half in, half out of a wardrobe. "Sorry!"

I bent down beside her. "What have you done?"

She knelt upright. "I was leaning on the base of the wardrobe and the wood gave way."

"Let's see."

She moved aside and I peered in. The floor panel had half fallen through. It looked like there was a space below.

It shocked me a bit.

"The wardrobe's got a false bottom." As I spoke a cold shiver ran down my spine.

"Wow, you don't think…" Kay grabbed my arm, her eyes huge. "Bella?"

"I hope not!"

"What are we going to do?" asked Kay.

I sat back on my heels and scratched my head. "Well, if we can find a screwdriver I could take the panel right off…"

Kay gasped. "You are joking!"

I wasn't. I got to my feet. "We've got to take a look now, Kay. Hang on, there's sure to be a screwdriver in the kitchen."

I guessed right. There was a tin of old tools under the sink. I ran back upstairs with a screwdriver.

Kay was sitting on the bed, knees drawn up to her chin. I had to smile. "Don't look so scared. Nothing's going to leap out and bite you!"

"We hope!"

The wood panel inside the wardrobe was in two pieces. I unscrewed the nearest bit. As I moved it aside, a kind of old, musty smell wafted out.
I pulled back and jumped to my feet.

"What!" Kay squealed. "What is it?"

"Nothing, it just smells a bit funny, sort of old."

I bent down again. Peered down into the dark space. What I saw made the hairs on the back of my neck prickle.

Something was wrapped up in a sheet.

CHAPTER 3
GLASSY-EYED

I stared down at it for a long time. Telling myself to pick it up. To unwrap it. But I couldn't.

Maybe it was nothing, just a sheet.

Or maybe it was Bella…

Kay came and stood next to me, hanging onto my arm. "There's something down there!"

"I know."

"Are you going to look?" asked Kay.

"I suppose…"

"Go on then!"

Goosebumps were all up my arms. Slowly I bent down, put two hands under the bundle. There was, without a doubt, something wrapped in the sheet. It wasn't very heavy, but too heavy to be just an old sheet. I felt a bit sick.

Kay backed off.

I carried it to the bed, laid it down gently. Then carefully began to unroll it.

Slowly, as the layers of cloth came away, I realised what it was. The sick feeling left me. I smiled as the last bit of sheet was peeled away.

A china doll in a silk dress, her eyelids closed, lay there.

Kay gave an excited little scream. "A doll! She was talking about her doll!"

I was so glad! And this was a real treasure. The doll was so old. Its china face had little cracks in it.

But that didn't spoil its beauty. It was so pretty, with rosebud lips and black curly hair that looked real. The doll was at least eighty years old. Maybe even older. Maybe it was real hair, I didn't know. But at least we knew who Bella was. Mystery over.

Kay picked the doll up.

As its eyelids flicked open we both jumped a mile. Then laughed.

Its glassy eyes stared blindly.

Kay checked it out. "Look, Lucas, it even has eyelashes. And its arms and legs move — and its head." She bent it forwards and from a voice box inside, the sound *Ma Ma* crackled out.

"This is ace!" I said, totally amazed.

"I love it!" Kay cried, holding it close. "Can I keep it? Please, Lucas, please can I have it?"

Ah, now that was a tricky one. It was Granny-May's doll. We really needed to see if she wanted it. It might bring back more memories. It could be good for her.

Seeing my face, Kay flashed that special look at me again and pleaded, "Please, Lucas. Pretty please?"

"It's not mine to give away…"

Her bottom lip pouted. "Well, you can't just chuck it back in the wardrobe."

"I'm not going to."

"And I bet it's worth a fortune. Doll collectors would pay hundreds to get their hands on this. It's antique!"

I suddenly saw why Kay wanted it. She could flog it on eBay.

I stuck to my guns. "Kay, we need to give it back to Granny-May. If she's not interested then OK, you can have it." I was pretty sure my parents wouldn't mind. Besides, Kay had been the one to find it, sort of.

*

That afternoon, we went back to the care home. The staff were surprised to see us so soon until we showed them the doll. Then we all headed over to where Granny-May was snoozing in her chair. The nurses came too, all excited by our find.

"Granny-May!" I said, stroking her hand to wake her. I felt quite good to be bringing the doll back to her. A real *blast from the past!* "Granny-May, look who we've found."

I held the doll in front of her. So it was the first thing she'd see when she woke up.

"Granny-May…"

The old lady blinked. And then her watery eyes fixed on the doll.

A look of horror spread quickly over my great gran's face. Her eyes widened until they looked ready to pop. And then she opened her mouth

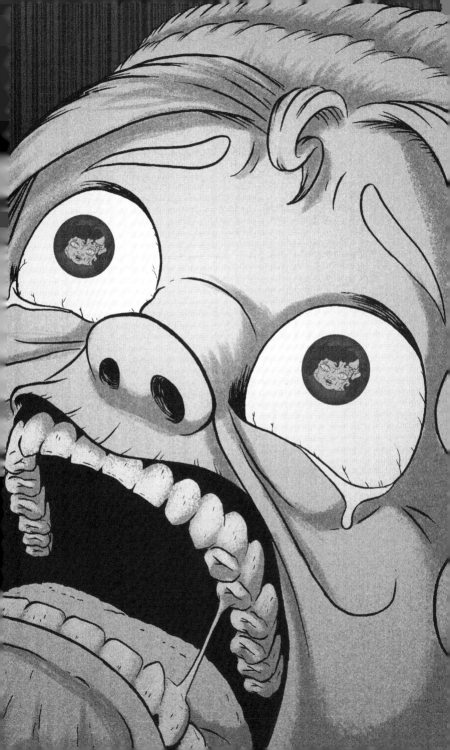

and screamed. Screamed like someone had stuck a knife in her. Her arms flew wildly, knocking the doll right out of my hands. Sending it spinning across the floor. Then she was up out of her chair, scurrying as best she could the other way.

"Keep it away!" she screamed. "Keep it away from me!"

I stood, shaking, too stunned to move. The nurses ran after her, grabbed her before she fell. They got her into a chair. Huddled around her, trying to calm her down. Someone fetched a tablet and a glass of water.

Kay looked at me with wide eyes. "Well that went well, didn't it?"

They had to sedate my great gran. Then they took her back to her room.

One of the nurses came over. She picked up the doll, smoothed down its silk dress and handed it back to me. "Your great granny will have a good sleep now. She'll be fine, I'm sure. Don't you worry, and don't look so upset. You weren't to know she would react like that."

I felt sick. I never wanted to upset my Granny-May. I really didn't.

Walking home, Kay took the doll from me. She held it like a baby in her arms. "So I guess it's mine now," she said, and smiled.

CHAPTER 4
TWO OLD PHOTOS

I played the whole thing down to Mum and Dad. I just said we'd found an old doll in Granny-May's house that she'd talked about. But when we took it to her, she didn't want it.

No big deal.

Ha! In fact, it was a very big deal. I'd never seen my poor old great gran so scared. And I felt really guilty for causing that.

Still, at least Kay was happy. She couldn't wait to get indoors with her new doll. I knew why. She'd be straight on the internet, checking out what it was worth. I bet it was up on eBay by now.

My folks were dead pleased with the tin of old photos. We all sat at the table looking through them. Mum tried to work out who was who.

"This is an interesting one," Mum said, passing me a faded old snap.

It showed a man and woman in old-fashioned clothes holding twin babies. There were four other kids around them. Big, happy smiles on all their faces.

"I think this is your Granny-May as a little baby," Mum said. "There were always hints of her being a twin. But never much said. I think her twin may have died young."

"And those four kids are her brothers and sisters," I said, wondering which ones were Terry and Susan.

"Yes," said Mum. "Your great-great aunts and uncles and your great-great-grandparents. My goodness!"

I wondered if Granny-May would like to see the photo. Wondered if she would know who they all were. Then I changed my mind. After the doll disaster, I didn't want to risk it.

Mum showed me another photo. "Look! Same people, only about four or five years later by the looks of it. There! That's your Granny-May and her twin. I'm not sure which one is her. They look so alike."

I looked at the photo. Six kids and their mum and dad. Granny-May's family. But… there was something about the photo that bugged me. Only, what, I didn't know.

And then I looked again. One of the twins was holding that doll. "That's the doll!" I yelled. "The one we found in the wardrobe."

"So where is it now, Lucas?" Dad asked.

"Er, Kay asked if she could keep it."

He didn't look pleased. "You should have checked with your mum first. It could be valuable."

"Oh, leave it," Mum said, getting up to make a cup of tea. "It's just an old doll. One thing less for us to worry about."

Phew! That was all right then. I didn't tell them it was probably up on eBay by now.

*

Lying in bed, I couldn't get the day out of my head. Sleep just wasn't coming. And I kept thinking about those old photos — the two showing Granny-May as a baby and then as a five-year-old. Something wasn't right. Maybe it was the doll, I just didn't know. But it was really bugging me.

What was it?

I started to doze off, still trying to work out what it was. Something was just not right…

I must have slept because, in the middle of the night, I woke with a start. Of course! I suddenly knew what was bugging me. To make sure, I tiptoed downstairs and looked at those two photos again. And there it was…

In the first photo, when Granny-May was a baby, everyone looked happy. Big smiles all round. But in the later one they all looked unhappy. No, it was more than that.

They all looked afraid!

All but one.

The twin holding the doll didn't look at all afraid. She had an odd look on her face.

And the only way I could describe it was 'evil'.

CHAPTER 5
BACK WE GO

The next day, Kay wasn't at school, and I couldn't stop thinking about that photo. Why had Granny-May and her family looked so scared all those years ago? And did things get better? I really needed to know. Was it something to do with the doll? It had freaked her out when she saw it again. Maybe it had freaked everyone out.

As soon as school was over I headed back to the care home.

I was so glad to see my great gran having her dinner, looking OK. I had a quiet word with the nurse first.

"How's my great gran today?"

She smiled. "No lasting effects from her wobble!"

"Good, because I want to try and talk to her again. About when she was a kid. Think I'll get any sense out of her?"

"Well you could be in luck," said the nurse. "She's been talking about Bella non-stop."

"Ah! No, Bella was her doll." I pulled a face. "You know, *that* doll."

The nurse frowned. "Really? I got the feeling that it was her twin sister."

I shrugged. "Who knows? Anyway, is it OK to have a chat with her?"

"Of course."

This time, thankfully, Granny-May didn't run a mile when she saw me. She smiled and called me

Terry. She was in a really chatty mood so I kept her talking, kept asking her questions.

"So, who are your brothers and sisters?" I asked, then to get her started, said, "There's Terry and Susan…"

"And Maggie and John," she said right off.

It didn't add up, there were six kids in the photo. "So who was your twin sister?"

As soon as I'd said it, I saw I'd hit a raw nerve. Her face changed. It kind of screwed up. Her eyes looked hard and angry. I just hoped she wasn't going to have another meltdown.

"Bella!" she snapped, and her false teeth clattered.

"Bella? Isn't that your doll?"

Her voice changed, like she was a little kid again. Back in the moment. "Bella bad girl. Bella stuck Mama with a knife."

"What?"

Her face pinched up. Eyes like slits. "And Bella hurt my neck. Her dolly bad too."

My skin started to prickle.

"Bella gone… Papa make Bella go to sleep. He put Bella and dolly in the wardrobe. She not hurt me now."

"No," I argued, for once putting her right. "Your Papa put the doll in the wardrobe. Not your twin sister."

She rested back in her chair, a peaceful look on her face. Softly she said, "Bella and dolly all gone now, all gone."

My head swam. If this was true, we were talking about murder.

I had to keep telling myself she was a mixed-up old lady.

Even so, I had to check.

*

I raced back home for Granny-May's house keys, then ran all the way there. My legs aching, and sweating like mad, I turned the key and went in. But now my feet dragged. I really didn't want to go looking in wardrobes again. Looking deeper this time. I didn't know what I'd find.

But I had to.

I went slowly up to the bedroom, the creaking of the stairs not helping. The house had an odd stillness to it now. Like it was holding its breath. As if it knew some terrible secret was about to be uncovered.

The musty smell wafted out as I opened the wardrobe door. Heart thudding, I moved the shoe boxes and junk from the bottom of the wardrobe. Then stared at the wood panel that I'd unscrewed before.

Feeling sick, I lifted it off. Stared down into the space. Nothing there…

But I knew I was only looking at half of it.

I got down on my knees, peered right under. Reached into the secret hidey-hole, my arm going deeper, to the very back of the wardrobe.

But it didn't reach the back wall. My fingers touched something soft. Something woollen, like a blanket. My heart pounded.

No, it couldn't be —

I closed my fingers around the blanket and dragged it towards me. It was heavy. Sick rose in my throat. I kept pulling until I could see what it was.

An old grey blanket wrapped around something. Something a lot bigger than a doll.

Just as I had done with the doll, I lifted the bundle out. I carried it in my arms to place it gently on the bed.

I felt like I was holding a child.

CHAPTER 6
ANGEL OR DEVIL?

I don't know how long I stood there by
the bed, staring down at the skeleton of a child.
It could have been minutes or it could have been
an hour.

She had been wearing a frilly white dress. There
was a ribbon in her hair — what was left
of it — and it was dry like straw. Where once
there had been a pretty face, there was now just
a skull with baby teeth and hollow eyes. Bony
fingers clasped together, and little white shoes that
did up with a button hung on bony feet.

She must have looked like an angel.

But Bella was bad, Granny-May had said. She'd stuck a knife into their mum and she'd hurt Granny-May's neck. I guessed Bella had tried to strangle her.

So Bella was no angel. It sounded like Bella was a monster. No wonder everyone in the family had looked scared. Bella must have been frightening the life out of all of them.

Her dolly bad too…

My great gran's words ran through my head.

Dolly bad…

An icy chill ran down my spine.

The doll was bad. Did she mean evil? Was there such a thing as evil?

Well, something had pushed this family to the limit. *Papa made Bella go to sleep.* Something had driven my great-great-grandad to murder his own child. Then hide her body at the bottom of a wardrobe.

He'd wrapped his child and the doll in blankets. Hidden them away as if they were as bad as each other.

Dolly bad…

Kay had the doll!

And Kay hadn't been in school…

*

I tore out of the house, not stopping to lock up. Not stopping for anything. As I ran, I tried to call Kay on her mobile. It just rang and rang.

My feet barely touched the ground and I wanted to throw up.

If the doll was evil — if that were possible — could it hurt Kay? Could it stick a knife in her?

I was being stupid. As I raced on, my lungs about to burst, I told myself I was being stupid. What I was thinking just couldn't happen. This was real life, not a horror film.

But in my head I could picture the scene. Kay lying dead, a knife stuck in her neck, blood and gore everywhere.

No! Not Kay.

I ran on until I reached Kay's house.

Gasping for breath, I rang her bell, banged on the door, hopped from one foot to the other, feeling sick with fear.

Then, at last, the door opened.

"Kay!" I almost dropped to my knees, seeing her standing there alive.

"Lucas! What are you doing here?"

"Why weren't you in school?" I blurted out. It was hard to talk. I was just so glad to see her. And I felt pretty stupid now for overreacting.

She shrugged. "I didn't feel too good, so took the day off."

"You're OK now?"

She smiled. "Feeling great!"

While I was so glad she was OK, I now had to tell her about the skeleton. I sighed. "Well, you won't feel so great when I tell you what I've found."

She folded her arms. "Oh?"

"Can I come in? I'm dying for a glass of water."

She stood there for a second as if she didn't want me to come in. "Oh, I haven't cleaned up yet."

I laughed. "You, clean up? You must be ill!"

"Cheek!" she said, flicking the towel she was holding at me.

I went in anyway. My throat was dry as a bone.
I went through to the kitchen, then stopped.

The doll was sitting on the kitchen table. Just
a doll, its blank, glassy eyes staring at nothing.
But that doll had been lying next to the skeleton
of a murdered girl for the last eighty years.
That made my stomach roll over. Kay would
be just as horrified.

I poured myself a glass of water.

A swirl of red rushed down the plughole. "What's
the red stuff?"

"Beetroot," she said. "Made myself a cheese and
beetroot sandwich. I told you I hadn't cleaned up.
Want one?"

I turned to see Kay standing there with a big
carving knife in her hand. A scary-looking knife
for cutting a bit of cheese. "Watch you don't cut
yourself with that."

"I'll try not to." She touched the blade with
her thumb. Her eyes locked onto mine. "It is
very sharp."

I don't know why, but the sight of her standing
there holding a knife made me feel uneasy, and my
blood ran cold. Granny-May's words jumped back
into my head…

Bella stuck Mama with a knife. And Bella had
owned that doll — that *bad dolly*!

My legs turned to jelly. Was it possible that an evil
doll could make a person do bad things?

Eighty years ago, had the doll turned a little child
into a monster? Could the doll work its evil on
others — on Kay?

All thoughts of telling her about Bella's skeleton
flew out of my head. My nerves jangled. I tried
to act normal. "Er… your mum and dad at work
are they?"

"No. They're in the other room."

I was so glad to hear that. "I'll, er, pop my head round the door — say hello."

There was more red stuff on the door. Red fingerprints. As if someone had stuck their hand in beetroot and smeared it everywhere.

"The beetroot's gone everywhere. Did you drop the jar…?" My words died away. Who was I fooling? This wasn't beetroot. It was blood. Bloodied hand-prints were up the door. On the walls. A puddle of blood on the floor.

I didn't go in. I couldn't…

Heart pumping, alarm bells ringing in my head, ice running in my veins, I turned back to the kitchen.

It's amazing how much your brain can take in, in a split second.

In that moment, I saw Kay lunging at me, arm raised, that knife in her hand, her lovely face twisted into an insane mask of pure evil.

And behind her, the doll on the table facing this way now. Its eyes glinting red. A twisted curve to its rosebud lips.

My last thought was that we should have left it in the wardrobe.

But it was too late now…

THE END

ABOUT THE AUTHOR

Ann Evans lives in Coventry in the West Midlands. She has written over 30 books, including the award-winning *The Beast*. One of her most recent titles is *Celeste*, a time-slip thriller set in her home city.

Her books for teenage readers also published by Badger Learning are: *Nightmare*, *Straw Men*, *Red Handed*, *Kicked Into Touch*, *By My Side*, *Living The Lie*, *Blank*, *Keeper*, *Promise Me* and *Runaway*.

ABOUT THE ARTIST

James Lawrence hails from a faraway land of vikings and motorcycles. He spends his days drawing rad pictures and chugging ice tea.

He is the creator of the fantasy wrestling webcomic The Legend of La Mariposa.